Oxford.

Pleasant Spots around Oxford.

MAGDALEN TOWER.

PLEASANT SPOTS

AROUND OXFORD.

BY

ALFRED RIMMER,

AUTHOR OF " ANCIENT STREETS AND HOMESTEADS," &C.

ILLUSTRATED.

J. THORNTON & SON
OXFORD 1985

Reprinted 1985
by
J. Thornton & Son
11 Broad Street
Oxford

ISBN 0 902672 65 7 (casebound)
ISBN 0 902672 69 X (Leather)

CONTENTS.

CHAPTER VII.

CHAPTER VIII.

CHAPTER IX.

CHAPTER X.

CHAPTER XI.

CHAPTER XII.

LIST OF ILLUSTRATIONS.

———

THE UNIVERSITY BARGE.

PLEASANT SPOTS AROUND OXFORD.

CHAPTER I.

"When daisies pied, and violets blue,
And lady-smocks all silver white,
And cuckoo-buds of yellow hue
Do paint the meadows with delight."

Love's Labour's Lost.

Thackeray—Isaac Walton—Town Enjoyments—Entrance to Oxford from Banbury Road—
Oxford Streets—Iffley—Iffley Mill—Iffley Church—Rickman—Oxford and Cambridge
Boat Races—Thames Floods.

HE writer who in graphic power is thought by many to be only inferior to him from whom the verse at head of this chapter is borrowed, has written, "There was a time when the sun used to shine brighter than it appears to do at the latter half of the nineteenth century; when the zest of life was certainly keener; when tavern wines seemed to be delicious, and tavern dinners the perfection of cookery; when the perusal of novels was productive of immense delight, and the monthly advent of magazine-day was hailed as an exciting holiday; . . . . when to ride in the Park

on a ten-shilling hack seemed to be the height of fashionable
enjoyment, and to splash your college tutor as you were driving
down Regent Street in a hired cab, the triumph of satire; when
the acme of pleasure seemed to be to meet Jones of Trinity at
the Bedford, and to make an arrangement with him, and with
King of Corpus, who was staying at the Colonnade, and Martin
of Trinity Hall, who was with his family in Bloomsbury Square,
to dine at the Piazza, go to the play and see Braham in *Fra
Diavolo*, and end the frolic evening by partaking of supper and
a song in the ‘ Cave of Harmony.’ ”

When Thackeray lamented the tendency of advancing years
to lessen our sense of enjoyment, he was not speaking his own
experiences : the exquisite descriptions of life and rural scenery
that often appear in all his works forbid such a supposition. He
is merely describing the changed tone that so often afflicts those
who will not sufficiently enjoy the delights that they can have
almost at their doors. The pleasures of a walk along the
Thames, or, indeed, any other river in England, are always
fresh, and whether we make our excursions in summer or
in winter, we always meet ever so much to gladden the eye.
Steam and excursions are apt to take us all away from our
native land, and much time is too often lost in a cramped
railway carriage that might, perhaps, be more pleasantly spent
nearer home.

The generation who lived before steam is not defunct, nor
nearly so ; many there are yet who can enjoy the pleasant
associations that are enclosed in the narrow radius of ten miles
that will include the drawings and letterpress of these pages.
Many, indeed, there are in hale health, who used to return to
their colleges after vacation in coaches, and to whom a steam
whistle would have been terrible ; and if the stringent laws of

Charles that forbad any country gentleman not being a member of parliament from spending his summer in London were in force with all their absurdity, the vivid picture Thackeray has drawn would lose its power. Isaac Walton had seen three-score years when he wrote his immortal work, and though doubtless his angling precepts may be very sound, as indeed they are, they are not to be compared in value with the pastoral parts of the book. Who cannot read with delight his poetic descriptions of country scenes to his scholar? Take almost any page :—"Turn aside a little towards yonder high honeysuckle hedge ; there we'll sit and sing whilst the shower falls so gently upon the teeming earth ; and gives yet a sweeter smell to the lovely flowers that adorn these verdant meadows. Look ! under that broad beech-tree I sat down when I was last this way a-fishing. And the birds in the adjoining grove seemed to have a friendly contention with an echo, whose dead voice seemed to live in a hollow tree, near to the brow of that primrose hill. There I sat viewing the silver streams glide silently towards their centre, the tempestuous sea ; yet sometimes opposed by rugged roots and pebble stones, they broke their waves and turned them into foam. And sometimes I beguiled my time by viewing the harmless lambs, some leaping securely in the cool shade, whilst others disported themselves in the cheerful sun." Now Isaac Walton could not only write this at threescore years, but nearly a quarter of a century after this he showed how keen his love of nature was, in a letter he wrote to his friend Mr. Cotton, on sending him a copy of "irregular stanzas," as he terms them, upon retirement, that had been originally given him by his friend, and which speak in quaint old rhyme of " valleys and mountains," "groves and fountains," but he says that if this offends

Mr. Cotton—though he has only added it as a preface to his work, that his friend's excellence may be better known, "and any reader that is blessed with a generous soul may love you the better"—yet he declares that if he is at all aggrieved with waking up their old pleasant days, he will, "so far commute for my offence, that though I be more than a hundred miles from you, and in the eighty-third year of my age, yet I will forget both, and next month begin a pilgrimage to beg your pardon, for I would die in your favour." Even if one may smile at the prosiness of the interview that would have taken place if Mr. Cotton had required it, we must always warm over the genial truth and friendship of Walton, and many of us may envy his keen delight in a country life, which he enjoyed to his ninetieth year.

Yet it is quite conceivable that in a healthier zone these very people might find pleasure in the million objects of nature that are free to them. Still, however, till they have risen to a purer atmosphere, "daisies pied and violets blue" will "paint the meadows with delight" all in vain for them.

The author whose words appear at the commencement of this chapter has given a very life-like description of the ending of one of these gatherings:—"As the party went down the great staircase of Gaunt House, the morning had risen stark and clear over the black trees of the square, the skies were tinged with pink; and the cheeks of some of the people at the ball—ah, how ghastly they looked!" And speaking of Pendennis the elder, always a favourite character with Thackeray, he says,—"What an object he was! The rings round his eyes were the colour of bistre, and those orbs were like plover's eggs; the wrinkles in his face were furrowed like deep gashes; and a silvery stubble like an elderly morning dew was glittering on his chin, and alongside his dyed whiskers, now limp and out of curl.

"There he stood, with admirable patience, a silent agony; knowing that people could see the state of his face (for could he not perceive the condition of others, males and females, of his own age?), longing to go to rest for hours past, and twinges of rheumatism in his back and knees; with weary feet burning in his varnished boots; so tired, oh, so tired! and longing for bed! If a man struggling with hardship, and bravely overcoming it, is an object of admiration for the gods, that Power in whose chapels the old major was a faithful worshipper must have looked upward approvingly upon the constancy of Pendennis' martyrdom. There are sufferers in that cause as in the other. The negroes in the service of Mumbo Jumbo tattoo and drill themselves with burning skewers with great fortitude; and we read that the priests in the service of Baal gashed themselves and bled freely."

Following up the same strain we might say that many of the younger frequenters of these assemblies only go as a duty, and drill themselves into obedience to the inexorable laws. Many a one who has completed the finishing touches, and hears the cruel wheels stop under his dressing-room window, thinks with longing of a party of friends who have made a boat of four to go up the Thames as far as Staines, spending two or three days on the water. It would be an act of cruelty to meet him at such a moment, and say, as Venator to Piscator in honest old Walton, "Come, my friend, let me invite you along with us, and let us go to an honest ale-house, where we may have a cup of good barley-wine, and sing old Rose ('Now we're met like jovial fellows'), and all of us rejoice together." What

a struggle between duty and inclination would arise in the
breast of an average Briton at such a moment, as he saw
his heartless companions roystering away and leaving him
solitary and reflective.

These reflections almost involuntarily occur if we revert to
scenes that were pleasant to us when country delights were
new, and enjoyed in the company of
some friend who has left a pleasing
impression in our after-life, and with
whom it is a delight to talk over bygone days. Cambridge has features of
its own, but the county round it is
more monotonous—the land speaks of
human labour in making the wilderness
and solitary place glad—the dykes, and
drains, and levels, and the superb ecclesiastical remains, that seem often to
be independent of outward wealth.
But the country round Oxford is more
genial, and reminds us of shady lanes
like those at Garsington, or Hanboro',
or Charlbury ; of historical sites like
Woodstock, Blenheim, and Abingdon ;

WINDOW IN ST. JOHN'S COLLEGE,
GARDEN FRONT.

quaint country towns; and beyond all, of the Thames that
flows through meadows of the richest luxuriance, and is fringed
with stately trees, and quiet, picturesque homesteads, and nearly
every scene that delights.

Of Oxford itself it is not our province to speak ; that
belongs to another subject; though we may remark, in passing,
that no city conveys a more thorough and immediate impression of antique splendour.   If we leave Trinity College and the

new buildings of Balliol behind us, after entering Oxford from
the Banbury Road, the walk along Turle Street brings us

ENTERING OXFORD, BANBURY ROAD.

into High Street. On the right hand is Jesus College, with
its fine Perpendicular chapel and shapely front ; and on the
left is the College of Exeter, which, next to Christ Church,

can boast of the largest number of members of any college in the city. Brazenose Lane is a remarkably picturesque avenue that runs down by the side of Exeter, and is shadowed over at the further end by the great chestnut-tree that is so well known in the university. Lincoln College, next to this, is not quite so picturesque; but when we turn down High Street, on the road to Magdalen Bridge, the view is magnificent, and has often been said to have the finest street vista in Europe. There is not only the grand Church of St. Mary's, but the Colleges of All Souls, University, Queen's, and Magdalen, that can be seen almost at the same time.

Grove Street, which we pass, is a veritable specimen of an ancient English street, and is hardly two paces wide at the entrance from High Street; though even this circumscribed limit is contracted overhead by projecting gables. On the opposite side is a lane leading to St. Edmund's Hall, which contains one of the most beautiful quadrangles in Oxford, and strongly resembles the court-yard of some venerable mansion. Some of these colleges convey a very just picture of what we might have expected to see in every county if the suppression of religious houses and the Civil War had not entailed the destruction of abbey buildings. These are nearly all picturesque ruins, unless they have been destroyed entirely.

The road after leaving Oxford and going towards Iffley is rather dreary, until the beautiful village itself is approached. There are some excellent houses just outside it, screened from the road by trees, and some very pleasant cottages, where the tenants seem to understand what a source of wealth poultry-keeping is. Opposite the " Tree Tavern " is an elm of astonishing grandeur, and further along the road is a very noticeable residence called "The Cottage," which seems to have been adapted as a residence from some old roadside cottage; the combination of a large bow-window with gables and porch and high chimney-stacks is very pleasing.

MAGDALEN TOWER AND BRIDGE.

If we proceed by road to Iffley, we pass over Magdalen Bridge, from which there is a grand view of the college tower. This college is dear in its associations to Englishmen from the resolute stand it took against the encroachments of James II., and like all other colleges, it has a list of

notable men among its scholars.   Magdalen Bridge is about
one hundred years old, and is a very imposing structure.
It crosses the Cherwell in two branches, and unites the city
of Oxford with the suburb of St. Clements.   This is a town
of itself, and has a population of more than five thousand
persons.   Magdalen College was built on the site of John
the Baptist Hospital.   Portions of
this still remain; and the first
quadrangle, entered under an archway, designed by Pugin, is called
John the Baptist Court; perhaps
the kitchen with its high oak roof
is a remnant of St. John's.   No
college in Oxford affords a more
striking picture of dignity than
this, with its venerable trees and
its deer park, and great pinnacled
tower rising up above the Cherwell
meadows; a tower from which it is
the custom to sing an anthem at
five o'clock on a May morning.   Its
proportions are very excellent, and

IFFLEY MILL.

its enrichments are good, though of course it cannot compare
in these with the gorgeous towers of Wrexham, or Gloucester,
or Taunton.   Cardinal Wolsey has often had the credit of
designing Magdalen Tower, but the style points to an earlier
period somewhat than his career.   Like all the colleges, this
can boast of a long list of distinguished names, from Wolsey's
downwards.   Probably, however, Purcell's name is as often
before us as any other of its scholars.   He composed the
beautiful anthems, "The greatness of Thy mercy reacheth

IFFLEY MILL AND CHURCH.

unto the Heavens" and " They that go down to the sea in ships," and many others of equal beauty.

Iffley Church is delightfully situated on the Thames, and the great square tower rises slightly above the well-known mill; indeed, so well is this mill known both by photographs and exhibition paintings, that it was almost a matter of consideration if it should be introduced at all in a work of original drawings. The scene here given, however, is from a spot where the camera would hardly stand. And perhaps the sketcher has many advantages yet over the most skilful photographer. On the rainiest day he can under some cover or doorway make a most accurate sketch, and fill in the sunshine and people afterwards; while the photographer's work under similar disadvantages would be, to say the least, not valuable.

Little is known of the history or origin of Iffley Church. John Britton, a very painstaking authority—almost a final one some would say—declares that, after much research, he cannot arrive at any conclusion regarding the founder. It was in existence in the year 1189, when Henry II. died, as is proved by documents now existing, and so far as style can be relied on, it would seem not to have been built at a very much earlier period. Deeply interesting the history of Norman architecture is, and its comparison with the Saxon which it superseded. Rickman, one of the most trustworthy of all writers on English architecture—indeed, the most trustworthy —points out some few distinctions between the two styles, and mentions some undoubted Saxon work, such as East Barton and Sompting Churches. He might, perhaps, have added some parts of St. Peter's, Oxford, where the Roman balustrade is very pronounced, and quite characteristic of the architecture

on Saxon missals; but in all probability the change from Saxon
to Norman was slight, and if we had the documents preserved
that would throw more light upon the dates of buildings that
appeared before and after the Conquest, we should find only the
same progressive architecture with which every one is familiar,
and that leads through steady and almost imperceptible changes
from the solid Norman of Waltham or Malmesbury to the florid
and fast deteriorating style of Henry VII.'s Chapel at Westminster.   Both the Normans and Saxons copied the style of the
Roman villas and cities, whose ruins abounded in England, as
there is every reason to believe, 800 years ago.   Could we see
a true picture of these remains as they were then, we should
almost regard it as the dream of an antiquary; but cities like
Uriconium (the modern Wroxeter), and many others that have
risen again from their ruins, were regarded as quarries from
which to extract building materials.   Many abbeys in Shropshire, Gloucester, Worcester, and other counties which the
Romans delighted in, show traces of the spoils.   They were
more cheaply acquired by this than by any other process.

Iffley is an exceptionally perfect specimen of Norman architecture, if the accepted indications are to be relied on.   It is
in wonderful preservation, and, indeed, the spoiler seems to
have held his hand.   It could not be decently " restored," as
the phrase goes, even by the most ruthless modernising
architect.   The few tinsel ornaments that have been added to
its grand interior are harmless; they can be removed, and the
building will remain as it was.

Britton, in speaking of Iffley, mentions some curious circumstances.   He cannot, as he says, after much care and
research, discover its true origin, and though Wharton ascribes
it to a Bishop of Lincoln in the twelfth century, he mentions

no authority for his opinion. "The Church of Stewkley, in
Buckinghamshire," as Wharton has remarked, "is exactly in

IFFLEY CHURCH.

the same style as that at Iffley, but with some variations in
the ornaments; and it is rather curious that the monks of Kenilworth were also the patrons of that edifice. . . The west

doorway to the church at Kenilworth is also very analogous in style and ornaments to those of Iffley and Stewkley."

All these buildings, however, are enriched with ornaments that may be traced far beyond any period Rickman has reached. The beak heads that characterise Iffley and other churches of the Norman period, seem almost to indicate a remote Eastern origin. I know of no enrichments like them on this side of the Caspian Sea.

The crypt also of St. Peter's, Oxford, has rude attempts to imitate the acanthus-leaf of the Corinthian capitals, though these are not nearly so perfect as in other places—Canterbury, for example, where the acanthus is almost as pronounced as in any column at Rome. Before leaving this part of the subject, it may be well to notice what has escaped remark—that the misappropriation of real Roman features shows that the work of the old settlers was in heaps of *débris*. Bases and capitals are sometimes misplaced, and at Sompting Church, which the painstaking Rickman ascribes to the Saxon period, Ionic volutes have been copied and placed in the tower arch, but though comparatively accurate copies of Roman work, they are placed vertically instead of horizontally, showing almost to demonstration that they were copied from broken pieces of ruins. Tiles were not so easily removed as columns or walls, and in all probability there are vast stores of these buried a few feet underground at such places as Chester, Silchester, and Wroxeter. At the latter, indeed, the raised site of the Roman city can be easily traced for several hundred acres.

The architects who succeeded the Normans were, as has been pointed out, always desirous to preserve the doorways, and hence we have so many admirably preserved ones in England; even when Tudor work has been substituted in windows and battlements, the doors are left. Iffley is peculiarly rich in that respect; there are three doorways of great value, and all differing from each other. The flowers in the south doorway are almost unique in Norman architecture. On the same doorway may be noticed rudely carved imitations of Roman centaurs. The cross and the yew-tree on the south side of the church are very curious; indeed, the yew is one of the most venerable specimens in England. In its hollow trunk a man, of no mean dimensions, could easily conceal himself.

The most pleasant way from Iffley to Oxford is along the meadows, by the river-side, over Folly Bridge, which is comparatively modern, being built in the year 1826, in place of an ancient one that was taken down. This old bridge was a very picturesque structure, consisting of three arches and a small culvert. A very accurate model of it is preserved in the Ashmolean Museum, and the remains of the old Oxford waterworks are shown in it at one end.

The college barges on the shore opposite from the pathway would strike an Eastern traveller as bearing some resemblance to Chinese junks; but they are vessels of great importance, and some of them have even figured in the Lord Mayors' shows. The University Barge was designed by a local architect, Mr. Bruton, and the Christ Church and Exeter have moorings at each end of it. The interiors of these barges are beautifully fitted up with reading-rooms and dressing-rooms. The annual boat-races between the two universities are decidedly among the most popular contests in England, and are more thoroughly national than any other. It is said that nearly every great annual horse-race may be open to undue influences, and that all coveted cups have at one time or another failed to fall to the best runner; but with the university boat-races no such apprehensions exist—every man does his best to win. If we take up a register of the races, we shall see how the honours have fallen. From the year 1836 to 1852 ten races were rowed, in which the Cambridge were victorious in seven, the Oxford winning in three. In the next ten years, from 1854 to 1864, the dark blues were triumphant in seven, the Cambridge winning three. In the next ten years each crew won five; then they won one each, and the following contest resulted in a " draw," the first time that such a result had been chronicled.

Continuing the river approach to Iffley, we pass by Salter's and Clasper's, the well-known boat-builders, over Sanders Bridge, and the two "long bridges" opposite the "gut," the limit of the Weir's Angling Society limits; and here again Iffley Church shows its tower through elms and beeches. The pollard willows along the banks are a great feature in the scene, and have a picturesqueness entirely their own. The Thames Conservancy House is a pleasant-looking yellow cottage, covered in the front with a large jasmine-tree, and on the front is a board which informs us that London is 110½ miles distant. The view of Oxford from any part of this road is extremely striking and grand, and the familiar objects to crews after leaving Iffley Lasher are the White Willow, the Freewater Stone, the "Stunted Willow," and "Halls;" these are the beacons to steer by, and mark out the proper course.

Some artists have a great fondness for mills, and, indeed, this is not surprising. They have always homely surroundings, and not uncommonly are possessed by men of substance, who arrange their byres and yards neatly. It is said that the mills on the Thames are the cause of so many floods, and that Iffley and Sandford Mills have their full share of blame to answer for. One ingenious engineer has assured me that the system of thorough draining has much to do with it, for where formerly the water soaked quietly into meadows, now it is carried rapidly by drains into the main river. Something or some one we think must always be to blame, but for all that there were floods in Shakespeare's time—

> "Therefore, the winds, piping to us in vain,
> As in revenge, have sucked up from the sea
> Contagious fogs, which falling on the land
> Have every pelting river made so proud
> That they have overborne their continents;
> The ox hath therefore stretched his yoke in vain,
> The plowman lost his sweat, and the green corn
> Hath rotted ere his youth attained a beard;
> The fold stands empty in the drownèd field,
> And crows are fatted with the murrain flock."

This graphic description would almost be absolute proof that we must look back farther than modern agriculture or engineering for a solution of floods.

TOWER, ST. JOHN'S COLLEGE, OXFORD.

DISTANT VIEW OF ABINGDON.

CHAPTER II.

"Sulmo mihi patria est, gelidis uberrimus undis."—OVID, *Tristia.*

Scenery from Oxford to Abingdon—English Scenery—Abingdon—Francis Little and Alms-
houses—Abingdon Abbey—Latin Records of Abingdon—Architecture of Abingdon
Abbey—Abingdon Cross—Richard Corbet—Boating Parties—River Thames and its
Tributaries—The Thame—Origin of Name—General Scenery of Thames—Natural
History of River—Fishes of Thames—Black Bass.

No part of England is more thoroughly English than the
road from Oxford to Abingdon, through the villages of
Hincksey and Radley. The Thames reappears at intervals in
the valley, and is lost again among great elms and beeches,
and there are many goodly farmhouses with tiled roofs and
gabled lights. The harvest was just stacked when this was
written, and the farmyards spoke aloud of wealth and plenty.
The trees at Radley are singularly grand and evenly grown.
There are no sea-winds to warp them on either side, and all the
elms throw out their branches indifferently in every direction.
An English landscape has peculiarities of its own that distinguish it from almost any other. Leaving aside its homeliness, which even foreigners admit, there is a pearly grey that
belongs to it alone. In the South of Europe the sky is intensely
blue, and the gradations of distance are not so clearly marked.

IN ABINGDON.

In cruising in the Mediterranean a vessel under sail stands towards a headland that she appears to be close to, and any novice going below will wonder she is not put about; but on returning to the deck again he finds she is still on the same tack, and the headland looks the same, for an hour to come, as ever. The same effect may be occasionally noticed in the West of Scotland, though not very frequently; but the grey veil of English landscape adjusts everything to its proper place. There is a paleness also about an American landscape, and though there are beautiful country scenes in Vermont and other States, they have not been settled long enough to afford the picturesque accompaniments of old homesteads; besides which the use of wood in buildings, especially when they have an external covering of boarding, hardly helps the artist; and as for log huts in the West, it is nearly impossible to form them into beauty, though they are unmatched in their power of resisting the heat of summer and the great cold of winter. No, the Americans themselves bear willing testimony to the beauty of an English landscape; and so thoroughly does its familiar appearance commend itself to them, in the Western and Southern States, where families have been settled for generations, they always speak of going to England as going home, and the English Government, even when speaking of a matter that may be in some dispute with their own, is commonly alluded to even then as the "home Government."

Abingdon is an extremely pleasant town, and a favourite holiday resort of Oxonians. The streets are irregular and picturesque, and they seem to have known but little change since the days of the Hanovers; and, of course, many of the buildings were hundreds of years old before a Hanoverian sat on the throne. The church is a venerable model of an English parish church, almost rivalling a cathedral in its dimensions, and its exterior is charmingly broken and irregular. A richly-painted roof is preserved here, which is covered with figures of saints and kings, and which, a somewhat doubtful tradition states, belonged at one time to Abingdon Abbey. But the great charm of the church is its picturesque surroundings; the

BOAT-HOUSE, ABINGDON.

fine old hospital encloses the churchyard, and there is all along one side a black oak cloister, spotlessly clean, and adorned with texts. This is surmounted by a high-pitched roof, and entered by some quaint porches. The "brethren" may be always seen on a summer's day sitting in the shade of it, and they look so pleasant and comfortable that many a one might almost envy their lot as they husband out life's taper, and enjoy their repose while approaching the end of, in their case too often, a weary pilgrimage. Past the gables of this retreat the Thames runs quietly on; and quite in keeping with the scene is the quaint little bow-windowed building shown here. It is very picturesque, and fills the uses of an inn and boat-house.

Francis Little, writing in the year 1627 of the founders of this hospital, quite warms with his subject, and speaking, doubtless metaphorically, of them after death, says, "For just and mercifull men are like unto a box of precious ointment, which, whilst it remaineth whole and sound, giveth little scent, but being broken delighteth all that are neare unto it with its odoriferous smell;" and he borrows a vigorous metaphor from the chase which shows he did not hold the theory "the evil that men do lives after them, while the good is often interred with their bones." "For," he adds, "their praizes which the envie of others suppressed, or their own modestie refused in their lives, after death follow them, as it were, with full crie."

Many are the learned disquisitions upon the origin of the name of Abingdon, and the site of the Abbey; and though there may be some obscurity in the matter, it seems to be generally allowed that Offa, the Saxon king, was charmed with the Island of Andersey, opposite the present abbey, and built a palace there, giving the manor of Goosey, on the Great Western line, in its stead to the wealthy abbots. The only conjecture we can safely make is that he must, perhaps, have been partial to the chase of the otter and pike. His son, also, we are told, was equally partial to the swampy abode, and lived and died there, though the succeeding monarch left it to his falconers and huntsmen, and found more congenial quarters. These residents had but little in common with the neighbouring monks, and their daily way of life was such that the recluses gave the king the beautiful manor of Sutton Courtney and a round sum for their removal.

The remains of the present abbey are very fine and picturesque, even beyond the most of monastic remains. They are converted into a brewery, and it is pleasing to be able to add that the present proprietors take great care to preserve them intact. Relics so left and so kept are a hundred times over more interesting than a modern restoration, and as for their superior picturesqueness, that at least goes without telling. In this particular instance monks' heads in massive stonework look down upon cooling-vats, and dray-horses are housed where the abbots' steeds used to dwell. One of the finest fireplaces in the whole of England is here, and it has occasionally been copied by architects in modern castles. There are two slender octagonal shafts, with massive Early English capitals, supporting a bold projecting breastwork, and the masonry is simply perfect. It has been engraved in a work I remember seeing, but the form is so little known (for the work has long been out of print) that it has been thought well to reproduce it in these pages.

The records of Abingdon Abbey are not written always in perfect Latin; indeed, the style of them is something akin to the turgid Latinity of the Vatican, though of course they have of necessity been the work of many scribes; and it is sometimes curious to trace the origin of words. The gradual relapse of Roman emperors into popes did not carry with it the purity and vigour of the ancient Roman tongue. The popes, whether they were anathematising the outer world, or whether they were bestowing attentions on each other from the Vatican and Avignon respectively, generally wrote in a facile schoolboy Latin. The will was obvious, but

ABINGDON ABBEY BREWERY.

the language exceptional, and one is almost reminded with a smile of the verse in the Ingoldsby legends where the " saint was uncommonly flurried—and apt to be loose in his Latin when hurried."

But all records are not kept in the same way. Those of Godstow Nunnery, so delightfully situated on the Thames, are quite an exception. This house seems, however, to have been out of favour with the hierarchy for the kindly way in which the nuns treated the remains of poor Rosamond.

Dogmatic Latin is a language *sui generis*, and the first syllable is yet commonly used to express a phrase or word of doubtful purity.

We read in Dugdale's "Monasticon" the deed conveying Cumnor Abbey to the Abbot of Abingdon, for his loyalty to the crown under the new regime, &c.—" Rex omnibus, &c., ad quos salutem, &c. Cum nuper monasterium de Abendon in comitatu nostro Berk. jam dissolvatur unde quidem Thomas Penticost alias dictus Rowland, tempore dissolutionis illius et diu antea abbas ibidem fuit, nos volentes rationabilem annualem pensionem sine promotionem condignam eidem Thomæ ad victum, exhibitionem et sustentationem suam melius sus-tendam provideri, Sciatis igitur quod nos in consideratione præmissorum ac in plenam satisfactionem totius pensionis dicti Thomæ ultra ducentes libras annuatim, ea de causa per quasdem alias literas nostras patentes, gerentes datum apud Westm., ultimo die Februarii, anno regni nostri XXIX. per nos eidem Thomæ per nomen Thomæ Rowland, datas et concessas dedimus et concessimus ac per præsentes damus et concedimus eidem Thomæ totam capitalem mansionem nos-tram de Cumnor una cum omnibus domibus, stabulis, horreis, columbariis et aliis cedificiis eidem adjacentibus et pertinentibus,

ac unum clausum nostrum terra vocatæ Cumnor Parke and
other lands, habend, for the term of his life, provided, that if

FIREPLACE, ABINGDON BREWERY.

the King do promote him to one or more ecclesiastical bene-
fices, or other condign promotion of the yearly value of two
hundred and twenty-three pounds, then these letters patent to

be void. In cujus rei, &c. . . . . apud Westm. sexto die
Martii anno regni XXIX. Par cancellarium et consilium
curiæ augmentionum reventionum coronæ regis virtute
warranti regii."

This abbot, Thomas Pentecost, *alias* Rowland, seems to
have been quite alive to the necessities of the times, and
acknowledged Henry VIII. as the head of the Church. This
prudence was rewarded with this " parke " and manor of
Cumnor, which was afterwards the property of the notable
Earl of Leicester.

The language of the deed of gift is simple, and almost
leads to suspicion that it was written by the shrewd abbot,
who wished to shelter his name under an *alias*, and was sent
for signature to Westminster. The abbey was broken up, and,
doubtless, the monks, who might have been consulted on
a knotty phrase in the classics, were no longer at hand. It is
said that his ready acquiescence in the new order of things
was not quite liked by them, and, if this is so, it is easy
to understand how they should have left him to his devices
when he put his pen to parchment. If he has ventured as
Cardinal Wolsey did, " like little wanton boys that swim on
bladders, far beyond his depth," he fairly feels his feet under
him when he comes to the main point. " Cumnor Park, and other
lands, habend, for the term of his life." There is no mistake
here ; the " habend " is judiciously subjected to an elision ; it
might be masculine, feminine, or neuter—and had not the King
quarrelled once with Wolsey on a Latin phrase, and that
too where all Oxford would say Wolsey was certainly right?
Plural the " habend " had a right to be, and that is, perhaps,
all that at the moment the abbot wished to make clear.

The gateway to the abbey, which seems to date only

from about the reign of Henry VII., and a narrow lane
leading to the abbey remains, are very clearly shown in the
accompanying illustration.   Other parts of the abbey seem to

ENTRANCE TO ABINGDON ABBEY.

be no older than this reign, and it is very curious to note the
encroachments of the Perpendicular style of architecture in the
domestic part of conventual buildings, and, indeed, others
of a secular character.   The necessity for economising height

where floors intersected the walls, suggested a flat head to the windows, and though that is freely copied in buildings of an ecclesiastical character, at a later period, there can be no doubt that such a form of fenestration owed its origin to secular requirements. At the back part of the abbey are some flat-headed windows, whose mouldings show that they are not late in the style; and, indeed, while those were being carved, some fine church windows of even transitional character were enriching parish churches. Of course it would be a fair assumption to suppose that nothing existing in monastic architecture can boast of a later date than 1536; yet it is curious to note the purer forms that may be found in churches of a similar, and even later period. And it goes without saying that careless design is generally to be found with indifferent workmanship; indeed, the remains of some convent that was built in the reign of the Edwards, will show better work of the Edwardian period—better and more truly dressed and jointed masonry—and much more honest mortar than it possibly can of the Tudor age. It is not too much to say, that very generally the thirteenth century work in any structure which ranges over mixed periods of building will be found truer and in better preservation than sixteenth century work.

The street in Abingdon shown on the next page is a winding lane that leads to the church and the busy factories of Messrs. Hyde and Clarke.

Abingdon is a favourite resort of Oxford men, and it is a pleasant row from the city. It may also be fairly recorded that it can boast of an exceptional number of excellent inns. Perhaps they may all have some merit, but I cannot help regretting that the tenor of the present work will hardly allow me to do more than allude to an old gabled hostelry not very far from the site of Abingdon Cross, that is a perfect model, in accommodation and charges, to all English innkeepers.

STREET IN ABINGDON.

So well, indeed, were one's wants attended to in this fine old hostelry, that in some of the journeys to Oxford which were required for this work, I went to stay with my old landlord, and travelled to Oxford daily; though, I hope it will not be inferred that any reasonable person can find fault with the hotel accommodation in that city.

The celebrated Cross of Abingdon was destroyed by General Waller, in 1644. There is a rude painting of it at the gable end of one of the almshouse buildings above alluded to; but we know more of it from other sources than this can tell us. It was not dissimilar in style and form to Coventry Cross, that has been so often described and drawn. There were several stages, and kings, saints, apostles, and prophets were niched under canopies, the whole being surmounted by pinnacles, crockets, finials, and other enrichments. Abingdon Market-house stands on the site of this cross; and I read in a very good guide to the neighbourhood of Oxford, that it is a remarkable building of ashlar and rough freestone: a description which perhaps it would be well not to enlarge upon. Dr. Laud, it is said, who was not even a bishop at the time, preached the sermon on the occasion of the reopening of the Abingdon Almshouses. It would be interesting to read it now, if a copy were extant, and see if the simple principles of Christian charity, which he so thoroughly forgot in after life, had any place in it. Surely this would have been a proper occasion to wake up any recollections of goodwill; for he had at least not been corrupted by place and royal favour. There had been no attempt to force any liturgy on an unwilling Church, and both Leighton and Prynne were in the full enjoyment of ears.

It is said to have been in Abingdon that Richard Corbet, Dean of Christ Church, lent a ballad-monger the assistance of his fine voice and handsome presence. This same Corbet was afterwards Bishop of Norwich, and was standing, Aubrey

says, with some boon companions, at the steps of a tavern
near the cross, when a ballad-monger complained to him that
he had had no success in his merchandise. The jovial
dignitary at once threw off his gown, and donned the leathern
jerkin, and chanted the verses with such effect that he soon
had a large audience, and disposed of all the ballads. Prelates
may differ considerably now from either Laud or Corbet, but
there can be no hesitation in making a choice between
these two.

The ferry-house already shown is also a tavern, and boats
are kept for hire. The steps lead down to the water, and
boating-parties have rarely much difficulty in finding men
to attend their craft, if they wish for a stroll in the neighbourhood. It is very gratifying to find how much these
boating-parties are on the increase from long distances. Any
day in July or August, or perhaps September, we may be
almost sure of meeting one at any hotel at Abingdon or
Oxford. The party of four have travelled from London, and
arrived at their destination, after several days pulling, happy,
hungry, and healthy, and that you are sure to meet four
" good fellows " is axiomatic; nobody else would ever think
of such a trip. And even if a previous year's work, either
at a bank or Lincoln's Inn, has caused the slightest accu-
mulation of bile, that will have gone to the winds long before
they reach Oxford. The great advantage of the journey here
indicated is that the heavy work is all at first—the pulling
against the stream; and after a well-earned rest, the road
home again is easy.

The fall of the Thames is not, however, very great. It
is about twenty-five feet in every ten miles from Oxford to
Maidenhead, and about twenty-two feet in the same length

from Maidenhead to Chertsey, and after this it gradually diminishes, till it reaches the sea. At Abingdon the Thames is joined by the picturesque river Ock, which runs by Stanford-in-the-Vale and Charney Bassett, till it reaches Abingdon, and it turns some half-dozen mills. This river is also joined by several tributaries: one from Wantage, one from Denchworth, and one from the northwards, which rises in Appleton Common. All these brooks are full of beauty, and might readily find occupation for an artist if he only were content to wander up them, and not indulge in reveries over Switzerland, and that even for the whole of his life.

The Thame joins the Thames at Dorchester, a few miles below Abingdon, and has almost more attractions than the streams already noticed. The country town of Thame is better known than the river on which it is situated, and the church is full of interest, with its brasses and monuments, and aisles and tower; but the quaint historian of Oxford, Dr. Plot, gives a poor account of the water that flows through it, and the wells that supplied it with water: which seem to have been so impregnated with sulphur that beer turned to a noxious compound in fourteen days. "At Thame," Dr. Plot says, "there is never a well in the whole town whose water will wash or (what is worse) brew; so that, were they not supplied by the adjoining rivulets, the place would be in a deplorable condition." Happily, canals and railways have, since Dr. Plot's days, placed them beyond the danger of his commiseration.

Many have been the discussions as to whether the Thames should be called the Thames or Isis in strict propriety, and often a compromise has been hit upon, that the river is the Isis above the ancient see of Dorchester, and that it adopts the

surname of Thame in addition to its own after receiving the
waters of the latter-named river. Camden is said by some
writers to have invented the name Isis, but it is clearly more
ancient than his time, for Leland, who was a somewhat older
writer, speaks of it, and indeed alludes to a still more ancient
authority than himself who uses the word.

The name *Tamesis* was used in Julius Cæsar's time, and in
Saxon chronicles which date back to the tenth century the river
is called Temise.   The following is a literal translation of one
that dates back to the year A.D. 905 :—

"This year Æthelwold enticed the army in East Anglia to
break the peace, so that they ravaged over all the land of Mercia
until they came to Cricklade, and then went over the Thames."
Now, Cricklade is forty-five miles above the junction of the
Thame at Dorchester, so that would go far to show the antiquity
of the name Thames in its upper waters.

The Town Clerk of Oxford has examined several hundred
documents that allude to the river, and some of these are of
very great antiquity, but in none of them is the name Isis to
be found.

The word Thames means "gently flowing," and in no way
is its character altered after receiving the waters of the Thame,
which enters it at almost a right angle just after leaving Dorchester.   There are other rivers in England that have the same
derivation.   There is the beautiful Tamar between Devonshire
and Cornwall ; the Tame in Staffordshire, which gives the
name to Tamworth ; and in Cheshire the word has been altered
to Dane—but it is a gently flowing river also.

If further proof of the greater antiquity of the name Thames
over Isis were required, the Chronicon Monasterii de Abingdon
may be cited.   In the first charter, dated A.D. 699, "In super

et de orientali parte fluminis Tamisa XX. cassator, quos mihi
Cuthredus regulus et Merciorum Rex Ethelredus necum et Ini

A CHANNEL OF THE THAMES NEAR ABINGDON.

rex Saxorum tradiderunt adjiciam X. quoque cassatos secum
vadus Bestlesford," &c.

The Thames meanders very much indeed about Abingdon;

as, for example, from Clifton Hampden to "the Cottage " in
a straight line the distance is about a mile and a half, but by
the river it is nearly ten miles.   In this respect it fairly rivals
the Wye itself, and the windings constitute a great charm of
the river.   Sometimes it divides itself into several channels,
which separate from each other for nearly a mile, and unite
again after draining many meadows; and these channels require
some local knowledge both to navigate in a boat or walk
along.   Often the pedestrian will cross some tempting-looking
wooden bridge like the one shown on the previous page, and
which to all appearance might be in daily use for many
travellers ; but he will find that it is a snare, and, after the
pathway becomes more and more dubious, it lands him in
a meadow or clover-field.   In these channels that are not on
a pathway it is surprising how many interesting birds and
animals we may find, and if we only sit down for a little, and
look around, they will soon learn that we do not mean them
any harm, and become quite familiar.   While the sketch of
the bridge here shown was being made, which was in vacation
time, two water-hens came timidly out, and hurried back
again on seeing an intruder ; but soon they reappeared a
few yards higher up the stream, and began to show that
he had no terrors for them ; indeed, it will occur to many
how these naturally timid creatures frequent the dykes that
run by railways in the fen country, and have ceased to mind
the railway-train as it thunders past them, safer, perhaps, in
their little pools than the passengers that are hurried by.   On
the contrary, however, we must all remember how often
martens and other birds were killed by the telegraph-wires ;
but now such a casualty rarely occurs; they have learned to
avoid them.   I have even on different occasions induced

snipe to let me watch them feeding, by keeping very quiet. Kingfishers and herons may always be seen along these water-courses if we only will take pains to approach them silently. Perhaps nearly every one of elementary education is now more or less of a naturalist, and, happily for mankind, if any person once begins to " dabble " in it, as the word is, he will find it very seductive—quite as much so, indeed, as ventures on cotton, or shares, or race-horses. " A little knowledge is a dangerous thing," Pope once said, and this aphorism has been so often repeated that there must be some sense in it. If, perhaps, an amateur chemist, who was only acquainted with the use of a pestle and mortar, were to officiate in a well-stored drug-shop for a day, and if he had a number of prescriptions to make up, he would be very dangerous indeed to his customers; but short of such an eventuality, the thesis of Pope is essentially and intrinsically untrue. The sneer also of Wordsworth at the geologist, who, when he sees some ancient fossil, gives it a barbarous name, and passes on, is equally unjust. Any one may, of course, be a most enlightened naturalist, as some of the trappers in the Hudson Bay territory are, without knowing the scientific names of the birds and fishes he has watched all his life long. Still, however, when there are such excellent systems for arranging genera, a single afternoon in mastering the elements of any branch is not lost; it saves much time indeed, and probably any one who has taken the pains to do so will soon become a naturalist in spite of himself. Observation, for which he has such abundant opportunities in the pleasant reaches of the Thames and all its tributaries here, is all he requires, and he will soon learn the value of many a stereo-typed tale that has been handed down from natural history book to natural history book, and accepted without any inquiry

at all. All round the meadows and hedges between Oxford
and Abingdon entomology may be studied, and collections
made that will in after years be a pleasure and value. I
remember reading a simple description of the differences
between a moth and a butterfly, written by a well-known
entomologist, that has made certainly more than one man
a naturalist. A butterfly, he says, always flies by day, and
always rests at night, while the habits of the moth are
generally the reverse, unless they have been disturbed. A butterfly when it rests perches on some spray, and raises its wings,
folding them back to back, while a moth closes its wings over
its body. Again, the antennæ, or feelers, of a butterfly have
two little knobs at the end, and they cannot stow them away ;
but the antennæ of a moth can be reversed, and he always
turns them under his wings when he goes to sleep, and so
protects them from sight and injury. And again, the waist
of a butterfly is contracted, making a division of the body,
while the moth has a full undivided trunk. Happily in
making collections of moths and butterflies a useful service
is most usually performed, for their larvæ serve no good end,
unless, as is said in some very few instances, they prey upon
other larvæ more destructive than themselves.

The fishes that frequent this river and its tributary
brooks are not quite of the finest kinds : gudgeon are too
small to be worth much consideration ; roach and dace
may be tolerable enough, if they are caught at the right
season ; pike are, of course, more valuable if caught when
the water is cold, and if they are properly cooked. They
should be stuffed with veal-stuffing, larded, and baked, and,
as all other fish, cleaned without soaking in water. This
is well understood now among educated classes ; but I have

seen cottagers throw herrings and other fish into a pail of water as soon as they were cleaned, and let them remain for an hour or two till they were wanted for use, by which time they were nearly valueless. Walton alludes to this in speaking of the chub, and insists properly on wiping a fish clean with a cloth, instead of even slightly washing it. Some of his finest passages may often be missed for want of careful reading, as, for example, in speaking of this fish to his scholar, when he expected he had hooked a trout, he declares—"Oh! it is a great logger-headed chub! Come, hang him upon that willow-twig, and let's be going." But, in the next page, he spies a milkmaid, of personal charms, and her mother, whom he remembered of old, and suddenly recollected the despised fish, which he presents, with a "God speed you, good woman! I have been a-fishing, and having caught more fish than will sup myself and my friend, I will bestow this upon you and your daughter, for I use to sell none." The ladies, of course, after declaring that they "love all anglers, for they are such honest, civil, quiet men," offer them some hospitality, and propose to sing a song, which is gladly accepted.

To return, however, to the subject from which we started: it is most probable that a new fish of great value will soon appear in the Thames, and it will most certainly become acclimatised—that is, the black bass of Canada—*Gristes nigricans* it is called by Agassiz; but its scientific godfathers have been too bountiful in bestowing names upon it, for it boasts of some four or five others. The English papers say that it is hardly inferior to the salmon or trout in game qualities; and indeed, after being for some years familiar with it, I should say that, if a comparison were made, it is a stronger fish, and more game to the last than either of them. Often, when the angler thinks that a two-pound prize is in his grasp, after a long fight, the fish will suddenly recover, and fight again as gamely as ever, frequently succeeding in coming off the victor, after having tried the tactics of his adversary.

Live specimens have come over into this country, and are just about to be introduced into the lower waters of the Thames. It cannot help but prosper, and will hold its own among any of the other fish it meets. They are commonly caught in Canada with a spoon-bait, and only one spoon-bait is of value at all: that is, the "Buell," so called after the inventor; and its peculiarity is that the spoon is detached, and spins round the shank of the hook. All others are apt to entangle the trolling-line in hopeless knots and twists, when drawn after a boat. Bass will also rise at a red fly, and then they give sport indeed. Any one who can capture a fish of two pounds with trout tackle will deserve to call himself a disciple of Isaac. They would seem rapidly to grow to half a pound in weight, or from that to a pound, after which the growth is slower, and they rarely exceed five or six pounds in weight. The latter may be considered the extreme limit.

Bass are very delicious as articles of food, and resemble a sole in its best season. An American book, called "Brown's Angler's Guide," mentions one very ingenious way of catching them. A youth having captured a minnow, hooked it lightly through the lip, and attached a red worm on the barb. Other minnows flocked round in time, desiring to make acquaintance with the one who seemed to be struggling with his prize. A passing bass, seeing the shoal, rushes among them, and they all escape except the one with the worm, which is swallowed by the bass, and it then becomes the spoil of the gifted youth.

The Thames at Abingdon is fairly cut out for bass, and the many brooks that join it would exactly suit him to ascend in spawning-time. All that is needed, when he is once naturalised, is some law to protect him in spawning-time; and then the waters of Oxford may rejoice in a new treasure. The Canal Bill shows that England possesses 4,800 miles of rivers and canals. A vast proportion of these waters are altogether open to wholesale fish destruction; but it is said that a few energetic men have been encouraged by high authority to seek for powers that shall place them under legislative protection.

Surely, if a new country like Canada places every fish, even perch and pike, under protection in its spawning season, we need not find any difficulty. We are as ten to one of their population; and as for our water surface, it is only a pond to theirs. Why, Lakes Huron and Superior cover a surface equal in area to England and Wales; and beyond the great system of lakes, others, not laid down on maps, some of them spreading over thousands of miles, extend far away into the wilds. But every fish is under the protection of the laws during their spawning-time, even in parts where it is hardly likely that the foot of the white man will ever tread. The Canadians are wise in their generation where fish and game are concerned, and they recognise their value. It is to be hoped that when their fish are brought into the Thames, they will also export some of their fishery laws. Excellently well these have been framed to preserve all fish but salmon, for which standing nets are allowed to bar the entrances of rivers, and stake-weirs are allowed to kill fish of immature size, during all the open months. Still, however, the close season has operated so well, in spite of these drawbacks—which have been abolished in England—that Canada could feed all its inhabitants on fish. And when, in due time, they have learned the value of allowing the free access of all fish to their spawning-grounds, and the mighty waste of tons of fry in the weirs, they will be able to supply England too. They have much to learn from us, in the item of capturing fish; and we have to copy them in the close seasons that protect every pond in spawning-time, from Nova Scotia to the Pacific Ocean.

ABINGDON BREWERY.

CHAPTER III.

" Ever witness for him
Those twins of learning, that he raised in you
Ipswich and Oxford! one of which fell with him, ...
The other, though unfinished, yet so famous,
So excellent in art, and still so rising,
That Christendom shall ever speak his virtue."—*Henry VIII.*

Abingdon Grammar School—Chief Justice Holt—Edmund Rich, Archbishop of Canterbury
—Birthplace at Abingdon—Tutor to Roger Bacon—His Study, Career, and Death—
Radley Church, and Road from Abingdon to Radley—Farmhouses and Stacks—Bagley
Wood—Autumn Tints—Return to Oxford—Nuneham Park—Harcourt Family—
Chancellor Harcourt—Mason the Poet—Carfax Conduit—Lord Harcourt's Order of
Merit.

DORMER WINDOW, MERTON COLLEGE.

ABINGDON Grammar School was founded by one John Ryse. Thomas Jeesdale was the first scholar, and he was co-founder of Pembroke College, Oxford. Scholars for this college were to be chosen from Abingdon Grammar School. But the glory of Abingdon Grammar School is that it can boast of the Chief Justice Holt as one of its scholars. This great man was born in the year 1642, and was contemporaneous with the worst king that ever reigned in England; he also had pleaded before the Chief Justice whose memory happily stands all alone for wickedness. Lord Campbell, indeed, says, in his "Lives of the Chief Justices," that he undertook Jeffreys' life with some alacrity, believing that he could rid his history of part of the obloquy that attaches to it. Nobody, he argued from his vast depths of experience, is as black as he is painted, and, in the instance of Jeffreys, he thought he was confirmed in this supposition from the fact that he believed no one could be so black. Little by little, however, his hopes faded away, and he found himself constrained to say he was not able to find one single mitigating circumstance to shed any ray upon his shocking career.

Holt's family was connected with Oxfordshire ; his father had a small estate there, and became afterwards Recorder of Abingdon, and he lived to see his son fairly enter upon his great career. Everything used to be against a defendant in a criminal suit, as it is too much now in France, where the law suspects any accused person of being guilty till he can establish his innocence ; and it was quite customary in England to interrogate witnesses about any man's antecedents, but Chief Justice Holt suddenly stopped the Crown prosecutor as he was bringing some circumstances against a man that had occurred three years before the offence of which he was accused. "Hold, sir, hold ! what are you doing ? Are you going to arraign a man for his whole life ? How is he to defend himself against charges of which he has had no notice ? How many issues are to be raised to perplex me and the jury ? Away—away—that 'ought not to be.'"

In those days of cruel criminal law it was quite usual to bring the accused party into the court ironed, and, on one occasion, one Cranburne was so placed in the dock. The Chief Justice, hearing the clanking of gyves, said, "I should like to know why the prisoner is brought here in irons ; if there was any danger of his escape before, there is none now. Strike them off!" That such a man was beloved by all the nation needs no telling. He also completely reversed the commonly-received ruling that a man must attend his own parish church every Sunday, saying that " churches were for the use of people, not parsons, and, if a man attended the service in Temple Church, for example, or Gray's Inn, how could he be at his parish church at the same time?" The often-repeated aphorism that " slaves cannot breathe in England," originated with Chief Justice Holt, but singularly enough, on merely technical grounds, as it appeared. The "Somerset case," that has been so often alluded to, was this :—A slave was sold, and the vendor sued for the amount in the Court of King's Bench, laying the issues at St. Mary-le-Bow. There was nothing in those days very remarkable in what we should consider such irregularity now, but the negro was described in the pleadings as "there sold and delivered," and the Chief Justice said, the action was not maintainable, for the status of slavery did not exist in England. If, however, he continued, the plea had stated that the claim was in Virginia, he would have been obliged to allow it.

Lord Campbell well sums up the character of this great man when he says that he was not a statesman like Clarendon, and he was not a philosopher like Bacon—he might well have added that he did not resemble him in other qualities less held in veneration than philosophy—and he was not an orator like Mansfield. Yet his name is held in equal veneration to any of theirs, and there are some who consider him to be the most venerable judge that ever occupied the seat of a Chief Justice.

However, our chief point of interest in Chief Justice Holt at present is that he was a scholar at Abingdon Grammar School for between seven and eight years.

There is a really good story told of him, which seems so
like a fiction that it would not be repeated here but it has
found its way into Lord Campbell's intensely interesting work,
on the lives of the Chief Justices of England, and that is
quite a sufficient passport for its reliability. In his younger
days he was travelling about Oxfordshire with a not too well
filled purse, and stayed at some hostelry where the landlady's
daughter had an illness that induced fits. She appealed to
him, as being apparently well dressed and educated, and he
promised to work a cure, which he did by writing some Greek
words on a piece of parchment, and telling her to let her
daughter wear the charm round her neck. Partly, perhaps,
because the malady had spent itself, and partly, it is quite
possible, from the effect of imagination, she recovered, and her
fits entirely left her. When the future Chief Justice, at the
end of a week, asked for his reckoning, she declared she would
take no money from him, as he had done her more service than
his tavern bill. Years rolled on, and he became the Lord Chief
Justice, when one day a very withered old woman was brought
up at the assizes for being a witch, and it was clearly proved
that she pretended to cure all manner of cattle-diseases, and
that with a charm she had wrapped up in a bundle of old
rags. She told her history of how the same had cured her
daughter ; and when the charm was unfolded and handed up to
the bench, the Judge remembered the tale, and recognised his
not very unpardonable escapade, and, of course, ordered her
immediate release.

But Abingdon was the birthplace of one who did more
than any other person to raise the character of Oxford University in the reign of the Edwards, and make it the resort of
scholars from the Continent of Europe.

In a small lane, which still bears his name, Edmund Rich
was born, some time about the year 1200.   His parents were in
very humble circumstances, and his father had sought refuge
from the cares and troubles of the world in the abbey of Eynsham.   This lies about nine miles from Abingdon, and is reached
by the wood that passes through Cumnor, which is about half-
way between the two places.   Eynsham and its cross are noticed
in another part of the work.   The cross, it may be remarked,
would appear by its architecture to have been contemporaneous
with Edmund Rich.   He received the rudiments of his education in a school belonging to the abbey, and at the cost of the
religious house ; his mother, we are told, was too poor to furnish
him with any other outfit than the horsehair shirt which she
made him promise to wear every Wednesday, and which probably
had been the cause of his father's retirement from their humble
abode.   Edmund devoted himself to the nobler life he found at
Eynsham, and soon he became its most conspicuous scholar.

He went from there to Oxford, and one evening as he stood
before the image of the Virgin Mary, in St. Mary's Church, he
placed a ring of gold on her finger, and as the language of the
time went, "took her for his bride."   From Oxford he proceeded to the great University of Paris, begging his way with
his brother Robert, according to the wont of poor scholars, and
on his return to Oxford he became himself the most popular of
the teachers there.

That he subsequently became Archbishop of Canterbury,
is of course well known.   But Oxford in reality owed her introduction to the works of Aristotle to him ; and many were his
eager scholars.   He is said to have made no charge for his
lectures, but any one handed him such fee as they felt disposed.
Even this he showed his carelessness for by throwing it on

the window-sill and saying, "Ashes to ashes! dust to dust!"
Among his scholars was one whose name is even better
known than his own, and who elaborated many of the philo-
sophies that Edmund of Abingdon had first taught him, and
that was Roger Bacon.

By Folly Bridge was the well-known structure called Friar
Bacon's study. It was taken down in 1779, and seems to have
been encircled by quaint gabled houses. An engraving appears
in all Oxford guides, and it must have formed part of a group
of wondrous beauty and picturesqueness. Among the legends
attaching to it was one that its owner had used such skill and
magic in its construction that it would have fallen on the head
of any one more learned than himself that passed under it.
From this was derived the common saying to any freshman
who came up to the University, "Don't walk too near the
Friar's Tower."

A similar legend is told of different towers on the Continent,
and sometimes we are furnished with a slight variation of it in
the world of Art. A piece of sculpture is shown with an unfinished figure, and we are told that the figure was designedly
left so, for the sculptor was the cleverest man in the world, and
resolved that his work should never be excelled, so that if it
ever should be, he could take refuge in the circumstance that it
was unfinished.

Bacon was undoubtedly one of the greatest lights, if not
the greatest, that ever shone—even in Oxford. The difficulties
he overcame in procuring the means to construct his scientific
instruments appear now to be incredible. "Without mathe-
matical instruments," he says, "no science can be mastered,
and these instruments are not to be found amongst the Latins,
and could not be made for two or three hundred pounds." His

history is very plaintive. After forty years of incessant study, he found himself, in his own words, " unheard, forgotten, buried." He spent of his own and his friends' money more than two thousand pounds—a very large fortune in those days, and ruined in all his hopes he took the advice of his friend Grosteste —renounced the world, and became a mendicant friar of the order of St. Francis. By an accident, for which we are now debtors, "a few chapters," written for friends, were brought before the notice of Clement by one of his chaplains, and he requested him to write a work. This was his *opus majus*. His friends had to pawn their goods to furnish him with money, for the Pope sent none, and £60 was required. Still, in little more than a year this wonderful work was completed. It formed an epitome of all the knowledge of his time, and suggested a complete method of reform in the modes of philosophy, showing why the progress had been so slow, and urging that sources of knowledge yet undeveloped should be worked out. He seems to have received no acknowledgment from the Pope, and having violated the rules of his order by publishing so much knowledge to the world, a prison was his only reward; and as an eminent professor of Oxford has well said, " The old man died as he had lived, and it has been reserved for later ages to roll away the obscurity that had gathered round his memory, and to place first in the great roll of modern science the name of Roger Bacon."

Radley Church is charmingly situated in the middle of woods. About a mile from Abingdon we come to Northcourt, and if we take the lane which turns to the right we soon arrive at Radley. If we continue our road through Little London and Kennington we emerge upon the Oxford and Abingdon Road without loss of distance.

The charm of Radley Church is that it has not been
"restored."   The architecture, which seems to be ordinary
Tudor, is left, and the additions of the Georgian period have
not been removed.   There is a curious monument in it to one

RADLEY CHURCH.

Gulielmus Stonehouse, who was a man of dignity, a "baronet-
tus," in fact, according to the facile Latin inscription on his
tomb. The elm-trees here are peculiarly grand and picturesque,
showing very clearly a long quiet life in a congenial soil.

Every one will be struck with the beauty of the farmhouses here. Some of them are commodious, and might serve

well for more pretending country abodes. One in particular will be noticed, with its red-tiled gables and attic lights in the high-pitched roof. Round this there were some noble stacks of hay that had not long been gathered in, and these were raised on stone piers to protect them from vermin, a custom which used to be common, and which, though still useful, is less necessary now than it was a quarter of a century ago.

Dr. Plot, in his amusing history of Oxfordshire, especially mentions the stone piers on which stacks were built, and seems to have regarded them as a novelty in his day.

Radley House is seen at intervals through groups of great forest trees as we go from Abingdon to Oxford, and before reaching the church there is a good view of a fine Hanoverian mansion, the family seat of the Bowyers, an old English house that received their baronetcy in the reign of Charles II. This residence has been leased to trustees as a public school, which is intended, though for a limited number, to supply the same education that the other four great public schools afford; and it has the inestimable advantage of being near the centre of classic lore. Indeed, when the wind is in a north-easterly direction, the Oxford bells are plainly heard. About a hundred and twenty acres are leased with this quiet abode, and those whose lot it has been to have received their early training there—and I have met with not a few in other lands—always look back upon the groves of Radley as recalling their pleasantest days.

Radley House was leased from the Bowyer family in 1847, and opened as St. Peter's College on the 9th of June in that year. It was founded by Dr. Sewell, who was for many years a Fellow of Exeter College, and not only a distinguished scholar, but one generally admitted to have been perhaps one of the most influential and successful tutors of his day. The ages of the pupils vary, as in other public schools, from about twelve to nineteen, and the number is usually about 130. There is, of course, a chapel, and dormitories, and a gymnasium, and, what should be part of every public school education, a swimming-master who teaches without charge. An admirable rule is introduced here that has been copied in other public schools where there is a river; a boy is required to be able to pass a swimming test before he is allowed to enter a boat on the river. This rule has been copied in Chester, and a boy that belongs to the Grammar School there must be able to swim in his clothes four times round the city swimming-bath before he is allowed to enter a boat on the Dee. The utility of this will be the more evident if it is stated in passing that I have been assured by the survivor of the wreck of a passenger steamer that struck the Scottish coast, that though any one who could swim twenty yards was saved, yet eighty persons were lost. At Radley, boys are admitted between the ages of ten and fifteen, and are prepared for the universities, the competitive examinations, the army and navy, and the Civil Service, &c., and the terms do not exceed those of Rugby. Radley may truly say, as far as the soldiers are concerned, "hujus domus, non pauci arma gestarunt nec inglorii." In the brief period of her career between the foundation and 1871, the School had trained a hundred men for the army, among whom are well-known names like Russell and Charteris; and three of its scholars have been captains of the Oxford eight.

Bagley Wood is situated about half-way between Oxford and Abingdon, and leads out of Radley Wood, which again joins the park of Radley House, so that there is a continuous

pathway through woods for more than three miles.   It belongs
to St. John's College, and is a fitting possession for the foundation which can boast of perhaps the most tasteful gardens in
Oxford.   Bagley Wood is a valued resort of the Oxonians at
nearly all seasons of the year, and Dr. Arnold declares that the
pleasantest of all his days were spent in it.   Here we find in
profusion wild orchids, and, indeed, every other kind of beautiful wild flower, and nuts, and blackberries.   In early summer
the blue-bells are in such profusion that the ground is car-
peted with them in parts, and to half-closed eyes it seems as
if the light streaming through the tops of the trees were
shining on still water that reflected a blue sky.   Of course the
autumn tints are not so gorgeous as we see in the woods in
North America.   But then at Bagley they are more sober
and less weird, and we know we are not on the verge of
a dreary winter that will lock the land up in snow for half a
year.   Dr. Arnold more truly expresses autumnal delights
when he speaks of " Bagley Wood in its golden decline, with
the green of the meadows surviving for a while under the
influence of a Martinmas summer, and then finally fading off
into its winter brown."   According to Leland, the abbey of
Abingdon was originally built in this wood; but it did not
prosper here, and was, in consequence, removed to Leukesham
and finished at the cost of King Cissa, who was buried
there.

The road after leaving Radley continues to be very beautiful,
nearly all the way to Oxford.   The valley of the Thames
spreads broadly out, and with its parti-coloured fields, shut in
here and there by beeches and elms, speaks aloud of prosperity
and comfort.   The river itself appears occasionally in a silver
loop, but is soon lost again in the foliage, and when we are

nearly opposite Sandford Mill Nuneham Park is fully opened
out in all its glory.   It is not that there is much in the house
itself to impose on us, as a specimen of architecture, though

NUNEHAM BRIDGE.

even here there is some amount of dignity and certainly of
comfort ; but the situation is so very grand when seen from the
opposite side of the river, that it would cover up any amount
of architectural irregularities if only a broad front were exposed
to the Thames.   If we take a fine situation like some we may
be familiar with, either at the English or Continental lakes, all
that an architect can do, or, if he is skilful, all that he should

STANTON HARCOURT CHURCH.

attempt to do, would be to present a surface for the eye to rest on. In the country the beautiful surroundings of a house are apt to stifle its architecture—while if the same building were removed to a town, it might have a better chance of being seen and felt. The Swiss bridge that connects the shores by the cottage is shown here by the engraver, and it suits the locality excellently well.

Nuneham Park is one of the most beautiful, not only in Oxfordshire, but in England. There is a road through it open to the public, and by far the most pleasant way of visiting it is from Abingdon. The road is very beautiful till some way after we cross the bridge, when it becomes rather more dreary, and the training college that was founded by Bishop Wilberforce in 1853, for training schoolmasters, will, perhaps, hardly leave as pleasant recollection of its surroundings in the minds of the students as the delightful streets of Oxford or the beautiful park of Radley. Leaving this on the right we enter the woods of Nuneham, and through many broad, shady avenues approach the Hall. The park covers nearly two square miles, and though it is enclosed, some few parts are under cultivation. The elms and other forest trees round the house are of particularly noble growth, and the view from the front of the mansion, which overlooks the valley of the Thames, was regarded by Brown and Mason as one of the most beautiful that any private residence in England could rejoice in. The gardens cover about thirty-eight or thirty-nine acres, and were laid out by Brown, assisted it is said by Mason. They were in great favour at the time they were designed, and have real and lasting beauties, but modern taste hardly regards with favour the introduction of so many surprises of statues, busts, and tablets. Gardens are intended so much for quiet and pleasure, that urns, temples, and flying Cupids are rather apt to give us the notion of being startled than pleased. The road which we are supposed to have entered brings us out into Nuneham village, which at one time stood near the Hall, but it has been removed to its present position on the Oxford and London road by Lord Harcourt. The houses are uniform enough, but hardly what can be called picturesque, and the church has no more interest in it than can be expected from one built in the middle of last century. Walpole has said of Nuneham that one " wakes in a morning in whole picture of beauty," if fortunate enough to be a guest, like himself, of the House of Harcourt, and this is doubtless a very correct epitome.

Nuneham Park is the principal seat of the Harcourt family, a house that has for long been conspicuous in English history. It would seem that the founder of the family was one Bernard, who was related to the royal blood of Saxony, and received Harcourt near Falaise from Rollo. Harcourt is pleasantly situated on the Orne, some ten or twelve miles before it receives the waters of the Oden, and at their junction the town of Caen is built.

Robert Harcourt accompanied William the Conqueror and fought at Hastings, and received the manor of Stanton, a few miles from Oxford, for his services. This manor was confirmed by Stephen and Henry II. to his descendants under the curious service, that the Lord of Stanton Harcourt should find " four browsers in Woodstock Parke in winter time, when the snow shall happen to fall and tarrye, lye and abide, for the space of two days ; and so to find the said browsers their browsing so long as the snow doth lie ; every browser to have to his lodging every night one billet of wood the length of his axe helve, and that to carry to his lodgings upon the edge of his axe; and the king's bailiff of the demesnes, or of the hundred of Wooton, coming to give warning for the said browsers, shall blow his horn at the gate of the manor of Stanton Harcourt, aforesaid, and then the said bailiff to have a cast of bread, a gallon of ale, and a piece of beef, of the said Lord of Stanton Harcourt aforesaid, and the said Lord or other for the time being, to have of custom yearly out of the same park, one buck in summer and one doe in winter. And also the Lord of Stanton Harcourt must fell, make, rear, and carry all the grasses growing in the meadow within the Parke of Woodstock, called Stanton, and South mead; and the fellers and makers thereof have used to have of custom, of the king's majesty's charge, sixpence in money and two gallons of ale." But the fortunes of the family suffered at the time of the Reformation, and it was reserved to Lord Harcourt, who was Lord Keeper, a title which was changed in his tenure of office, in the year 1713, to Lord Chancellor to restore them.

Many Harcourts had flourished in the meantime; one had been standard-bearer to Henry VII., at the battle of Bosworth Field; and one had been an adventurous explorer, with Sir Walter Raleigh, of Guiana and other parts; and members of the family had repeatedly sat in Parliament and occupied the office of High Sheriff for the county.

The Chancellor was the son of Sir Philip Harcourt by the daughter of Sir William Waller, the Parliamentarian general who besieged Basing House, and was one of the most conspicuous generals of the time until Cromwell himself and Fairfax appeared on the scene. For though he was beaten in three successive assaults on the Marquis of Winchester's castle, he acquired for himself among the soldiery the name of "William the Conqueror."

Harcourt was born in 1660, and entered Pembroke College—then not a very old foundation—the same college where Pym, Dr. Johnson, and Tom Hood were scholars. He was like the father of the great Chief Justice Holt, Recorder of Abingdon, and he represented it for some time in Parliament. He seems to have sat for it first in the year 1690, and to have retained his seat during the whole of the reign of William III. He was remarkable for his wit, and eloquence, and ability, and these were mentioned in addition to his legal abilities as qualifying him to take his place among the peerage when his claims were first preferred.

It is somewhat singular ·that, while he was Solicitor-General, he was also Chairman of the Buckinghamshire Quarter Sessions, and some of his addresses to the Grand Jury are yet preserved in the British Museum. It rarely happens that such a post has been so very suitably filled ; indeed, he was more eminently qualified for this honour than some of the more prominent ones that fell to his lot. Harcourt was elected for Abingdon in the year 1708, and his return was petitioned against by the Whigs. There was a sort of poetic justice in the result. He was a strong Tory, and it was about now that the names of Whig and Tory first began to be generally used as distinctive of party in any considerable degree. According to Roger North the friends and supporters of James II. were called Yorkists, but the name did not scandalise or reflect enough. "Then they came to 'Tantivy,' which meant riding post to Rome." The Duke of York favoured Irishmen, at which the candid chronicler says that his friends "were straight become Irish, and so wild Irish, thence Bogtrotters, and in the *copia* of the factious language the word Tory was entertained, which signified the most despicable savages among the wild Irish, and being a vocal, clear-sounding word, readily pronounced, it kept hold, and took possession of the foul mouths of the faction." The Tories were not to be outdone in the item of epithets, and we learn from the old chronicler that Whig was the Scotch word for " sour whey," and that seemed to be a suitable designation in their eyes for their opponents. So high did these faction strifes run in Queen Anne's days, that Dr. Sacheverell converted the pulpit into a kind of arena for the expression of extreme Tory views, and took a journey through England, to advocate them. This journey was a perfect triumph, but he was impeached by the Whigs then in power, and his defence was entrusted to Harcourt. This task was easy. He showed that his client was a fanatical, harmless person, and all unworthy the prominence that his adversaries had given him by proceeding to such lengths, and of course he was virtually acquitted. The absurdity of the trial led to the downfall of the Whigs. The election of Harcourt for Abingdon, however, in 1708, was petitioned against, and he himself had started the theory that those in power should use their power for their own benefit. This told against him, for though there was undoubtedly a majority of legal votes in his favour, his own principle was fatal to his claims ; and not very long afterwards the Duke of Marlborough removed him from the stewardship of Woodstock.

When the Tories returned to power, he sat again for Abingdon ; but, before he took his seat, the Great Seal was delivered into his hands. The title of the holder of the Great Seal was the Lord Keeper, but during his tenure of office the present title of Lord Chancellor was substituted for it. He signed all formal proceedings relating to the reign of the House of Hanover; but it was suspected that he secretly favoured the plots of Atterbury and Bolingbroke to secure the return of the Stuart dynasty to power. He did not fare so ill as Bolingbroke, but the day after the king entered London he dismissed the Lord Chancellor from his office. He entirely, however, changed his politics, and became as fully a Hanoverian as Sir Robert Walpole—a turn which caused him to be branded with the epithet, "Trimmer." He survived George I. only two months, and died in Cavendish Square—then in the zenith of its day—and was conveyed to the family burial-place at Stanton Harcourt.

Lord Harcourt was never a great judge, and his decisions are seldom quoted now as authoritative. His grandson, Simon, was created an earl by George II., and he was succeeded by his son Simon. Simon had no issue, and was succeeded by his brother, General William Harcourt. He was a personal and valued friend of George III., who occasionally visited him at Nuneham. He died in the year 1830, and then the title became extinct. The Archbishop of York, Edward Vernon, was a maternal nephew, and on the demise of his uncle he succeeded to the large estates of the Harcourt family, and assumed the name and arms of Harcourt.

Mason, the poet, who, with Capability Brown, assisted to lay out the gardens of Nuneham, was a man of some ability, though his works are not very much read now. Perhaps the inscription which he wrote for his wife's tomb in Bristol Cathedral is as well known as any of his poems :—

> "Bid them be chaste, be innocent like thee,
> And if so fair, from vanity as free."

The whole epitaph, however, of some length, is beautifully

written. Mason entered St. John's College, Cambridge, and in 1745 he took his first degree. Possibly the beauty of the grounds there, combining with those of Trinity College, may have first turned his attention to landscape gardening. Mason's " Isis " was formerly a well-known poem, and written against the supposed Jacobitism that was believed to prevail at Oxford; and this gave rise to Wharton's "Triumph of Isis." Mason attempted to restore the ancient Greek chorus in tragedy; but he seems to have failed in this completely: the chorus was too exotic for our island. His "English Garden," of which the first edition appeared in the year 1772, was much more successful. It was a descriptive poem of an English garden, and justly enjoyed some celebrity. All Mason's sympathies were with the Americans at the breaking out of the war with England. He was as staunch as Pitt, or any other minister on the Opposition side, and wrote several powerful appeals in their favour, but in vain. Singularly enough, however, he lived to recant his opinions in favour of republicanism, in consequence of the extremes he saw afterwards in the French Revolution. Mason was sufficiently recognised as a poet to secure his memorial being placed in Westminster Abbey in the Poet's Corner. He was, in addition to his skill as a gardener and scholar, a very accomplished musician, and held the post of precentor to York Cathedral for thirty-two years.

Carfax Conduit, which is here shown, was removed from Carfax, in Oxford, and was one of the conduits that were such ornaments to towns and cities in former years. There is one at Lincoln, of much earlier date, and one at Sherborne, in Dorset; and a celebrated one at Wells has been engraved in Britton's "Picturesque Antiquities of English Cities."

This one was built by Otho Nicholson, whose initials it bears, and it was removed to Nuneham, in 1787, by Simon, Lord Harcourt, to his park at Nuneham. Skelton says that it was removed from its present site to Nuneham under the

CARFAX CONDUIT.

authority of the Paving Act, and adds, " Few ancient conduits are preserved in England ; there is one in the centre of the great court at Trinity College, Cambridge ; a situation so appropriate that we are at a loss to conjecture what prevented the liberal founder of this from placing it in a corresponding part of the college of which he was a member, or why it was not suffered to occupy that situation afterwards, instead of its being removed to so great a distance, especially as the fountain now in the centre of the Quadrangle of Christ Church is supplied by a pipe from the same water;" and though visitors have no trouble in seeing it where it now is, one can hardly fail to sympathise with Skelton's suggestion. Lord Harcourt, it is said, established an order of merit among his tenantry, similar to the village fêtes in the North of France. They assembled in the parish church, where he and Lady Harcourt were seated on a high daïs, and distributed the rewards to the best-conducted of them. The names were painted on the walls of the church, and a large "M" was placed opposite each.

No doubt there were many advantages in this order, but the danger often is to make the holders regard themselves so very unduly superior to their neighbours. It is hardly like an agricultural prize, where turnips can be weighed, and one root fairly matched against another; but the test of merit seems to have been rather too arbitrary. And when on this subject it may not be quite out of place to remark that at Knutsford—a beautiful village not many miles from where these lines are written—the old ceremony of raising the maypole, and dancing round it, is continued to the present time, and attracts many visitors from even distant parts. Here again there is an order of merit, and the Queen of the May is the most successful Sunday-school scholar. Perhaps this is rather an improvement on the old test of comeliness, for if Tennyson's "little Alice" had lived she would have been very intolerable in about a year, at least, if we may judge from her many remarks about herself that she utters in the "May Queen" and "New Year's Eve." An

unpleasant suspicion rather lurks about, after reading the
three odes she is supposed to utter, that she was a young
lady of robust health, and may be alive yet.

Sandford Mill has undergone some recent alterations, but
every one will recognise the illustration here given. "Training
ale," as it is called, is posted up on a signboard very conspicuously; but most athletes will agree that for any feat of
rowing or walking even the most suitable malt liquor should
be used circumspectly. Many curious and interesting facts
were being established regarding the powers of endurance of
the human body, and the best ways of encountering strain
were being solved when the institution called the "Ring"
was suppressed. Among others it was found that for any
excessive strain in prospect the human frame could be trained
up to a certain point of excellence, each one according to the
measure allotted it ; but if brought up to the highest possible
point of training the condition was abnormal, and could not
be sustained for more than some twenty-four hours! This,
of course, shows that only a certain amount of training is good
for any one who is not called on to perform some athletic feat.
These are subjects, of course, on which the medical profession
are hardly called on to decide, or to offer any opinion on—
it is more the ailments of humanity that it is their grateful
province to deal with. Sandford Pool is reckoned extremely
dangerous, and has proved fatal to many a promising student
from Oxford. Dangerous it should not be if proper knowledge were used in the management of skiffs, and those who
doubt this should only see the great ease with which the
habitans, or the half-bred Indians, in Canada can steer a
frail canoe through miles of white foaming rapids. "Only
keep still," they say, unless, which is hardly probable, the

white traveller has skill enough to assist them in climbing or descending rapids. Should he not have this skill, he will see his dusky pilot, while he reclines in the bottom of the canoe, patiently fix his boat-hook on the rocks below, and push the tiny birch-bark craft up noisy rapids, while hundreds

SANDFORD MILL.

of thousands of tons of water are thundering past on either side. There is much picturesqueness in the grouping of the buildings and in the bridge here; but, probably, the preference would be given to Iffley for beauty.

The Thames and the railway may both be crossed at Sandford, and a delightful walk, either through Kennington or Radley Wood, will bring us back to Oxford. Of course,

the entrance to the city from here is not so imposing as
that from Nuneham over Magdalen Bridge; but it is very
quaint and interesting, there are many old-fashioned gables
and projecting storeys, and some great stacks of chimneys.
There are not a few Tudor doorways, with remains of carving
on the lintels. St. Aldate's Church also is full of interest,
and is said to have been originally built of wood in the
middle of the sixth century. The present building, however,
is ancient; some parts of it are coeval with the Norman
Conquest, and there are additions of the period of the fourteenth century.

We pass by the gateway also of Pembroke College, under
which, according to Macaulay, Dr. Johnson used often to
be seen in the last century in the midst of a group of scholars,
over whom, in spite of his tattered gown and doubtful linen,
he had great influence. Opposite this is Christ Church, where
Wellington, Peel, and Gladstone were students, and a whole
host of eminent men besides.

MAGDALEN CLOISTERS.

CHAPTER IV.

"The ceiling fine, and carvèd boards,
    With all the goodly stones—
With axes, hammers, bills, and swords
    They beat them down at once."
                    Sternhold and Hopkins.

Road from Abingdon to Dorchester—Long Wittenham—Clifton Hampden Church Restoration —Dorchester—Ancient Stone Crosses—Effigies—Danes at Dorchester—Richard Beau-forest—Jonathan Bradford—Steventon—Alien Priory—Sir Hugh Calveley—Anselm : Dyke Hills—Milton Church—Milton Mill—Sutton Courtney—Water-power.

OXFORD is liberally supplied with railway accommodation. There are no less than six lines that issue from it in different directions. In a few minutes, therefore, the pedestrian may place himself on new ground, and glide over that with which he is more familiar. Wheatly or Culham or Abingdon are excellent starting-points from the south and east, while Yarnton, Eynsham, or Islip are equally convenient for the north and west.

If we proceed by rail then to Culham or Abingdon, we shall be conveniently placed to explore Steventon, Sutton Courtney, or Dorchester. Culham is, of course, more central, but Abingdon is by far the pleasanter starting-point.

The road from Abingdon to Dorchester is very beautiful, and lies through fertile lands and past pleasant homesteads. Shade-trees, elms and beeches, line each side of the way after passing the Thames bridge, and often meet over the high-road. Perhaps it is not too much to say that every scene in England has its charms at each season of the year, and those who cannot see something to enjoy even in a "Scotch" mist, as it is called—though it visits every part of the island with great regularity—are not quite alive to their privileges.

But the time when the sketches were made that figure here was exceptionally pleasant—the early part of July. All the Phyllises and Corydons, as the poets of last century termed the farm-labourers of the period, were making hay or stacking it, or gathering fruit for the Oxford market. When the second milestone is passed, the landscape is much broader; the rich valley of the Thames is bounded by the Berkshire hills; and in summmer weather these have the pearly grey look that cannot be seen out of England. I hardly know any other way to describe it, even after years of observation; but the grey pearly tint pertains to England, and happily the walls of our Academy show that it is not difficult to imitate with success. Indeed, the rooms of the two water-colour societies bear even stronger witness to that, and speak in a material that is more suitable to represent it. The newly-cut hay-fields, and the ripening grain, formed a fine contrast to the elms and beeches that rise at intervals in purple-black, and all the rural popula-tion were engaged either in carting hay or putting the finishing touches to the thatching of the stacks. Homesteads looked so peaceful, and so free from care, that with their garden patches and bee-hives they spoke more eloquently in praise of a country life than all the poets that ever sang. It is pleasant also to be able to say that the new agricultural machines, with their unwonted but not unmusical sound, do not interfere with the beauty of the landscape, as indeed it might have been presumed they would. The tall winnowing-machine, as it rises from the stack-yard, and seems to make the rustics even more deliberate than ever, is no unpleasant object, and besides this it may be generally said to bespeak good husbandry. A well-kept farm-

yard is more pleasant to look at than a slovenly one, and an
artist who requires broken-down sheds to make his works
picturesque has not arrived at the highest point of his profession.   Ruskin in one of his works has made this very clear.

LONG WITTENHAM CHURCH.

He gives etchings of two windmills, one by Stanfield, and one
by Turner; the former is dilapidated, and the other in perfect
working order.   At first sight he truly says any one might
prefer the former, but on a more intimate acquaintance with
them, the latter, from the associations that gather round it,
becomes of necessity more pleasing.   Take, again, Morland's

pictures : true they may be to nature, and clever; but one too often feels a pity for the animals that live in his farmyards, and a decided wish that their keepers had been born under the workings of the Education Act.   Are Landseer's animals less picturesque ?   Nothing here can for a moment be supposed to apply to grey old buildings, which are strong and sturdy, and have greater life in them than a dozen new ones; indeed, the too frequent essays to modernise ancient churches belong to a very different subject.

The pleasantest way to Dorchester is to cross the river at Clifton Hampden, and wander along the Thames to Wittenham, leaving Long Wittenham on the left.

Clifton Hampden is a delightful village, nestling in great shade-trees, and the church was of more than ordinary beauty and interest.   The Thames winds placidly by, past elms and beeches, and under willows, and every little bay where there is still water is covered with yellow lilies.   On a summer's day, when the water is clear, any one going quietly to the bank will see great numbers of fish—bream, roach, and carp.   Some of these may often be noticed of great size, almost approaching the monsters in the pond in Christ Church quadrangle in Oxford.

The Church of Clifton Hampden has suffered from the " restorer," as have too many others in the country, and one sometimes is almost in despair of " restoration " being called by its proper name—destruction.   Fortunately, in this particular church the dim light which its original builders designed for it hides much of the decoration of the interior; but some architect—a " restorer," it was said—has laid his heavy hand upon it.   " Surely you would not let the old churches go to decay ? " I fancy some one may add.   Most certainly not ; keep

THE THAMES AT CLIFTON HAMPDEN.

them in thorough repair, but understand what that really means. A limb, for example, may be so injured as to require immediate and thorough treatment, even possibly for the safety of the body itself; and to remove it, and supply its place with a modernly-contrived substitute, is unquestionably the work of a man of skill. But how can his skill compare with that of another practitioner's who, combining a greater knowledge of his profession with more anxious care, can restore the uses of the limb to its owner? Yet this is understating the case, for sometimes so happy an issue as the latter is impossible. In the case of buildings, however, it is not too much to say that every one which has had its ancient features obliterated in the work of restoration, might have been preserved in its entirety. A passer-by should never have known that the "restorer" had been at work, and many a pleasant old abbey-church or cathedral would have looked as it did to our fathers.

Appliances are at hand on every side; all that is wanting is scientific knowledge on the part of architects; and this is said by one who has not only served his time to the profession, but worked with plane and trowel among artisans, in order to arrive at a more complete knowledge of the craft. Look at the Layard Ivories in the British Museum; how were they kept together, and what was their age? One might say with Horace Smith, in his "Address to the Mummy," "Antiquity appears to have begun long after thy primeval race was run." These were, however, treated by men of science, and by a beautiful process restored to their ancient condition, and that when a touch would have crumbled them. How such care compares with the destruction of cathedrals and parish churches that seems now to be the rage! A few years ago a Scotchman

succeeded so well in describing his grievances when visiting
Iona that the *Times* published his complaint. His enthusiasm
had warmed, and he was profitably contemplating the effigies
of some of the Scottish monarchs, when two Southerners
landed, either from a yacht or steamer, and "prodded," as
he plaintively said, some of the kings with their umbrellas,
remarking at the time, "Rum old things, ain't they?" No
one can, it is to be hoped, deny him sympathy for the rude
check to his meditations, yet his grievance was not so great as
those we are considering. The English visitors would most
probably not stay very long, and he could then continue
his reflections almost from where he left off. What would
he have said if his monarchs had been removed, perhaps
broken up for foundations to new tombstones with modern
figures; or supposing that Duncan, after life's fitful fever, when
he should have been sleeping well, was "restored," and placed
on a marble slab with gaiters and ruffles (for restorers are not
nice as to accuracy in details), and glass eyes added from a
naturalist's? Supposing treason really had done his worst, and
no steel nor poison could touch him further, what would he
have then said? Yet the treatment here indicated is only a
fair analogy to that which we have all seen again and again,
and to the ruin which is now unhappily going on in more than
half the counties in England. What a monument any bishop
would deserve who said, when he was applied to for a "faculty"
to allow a church to be restored, "What do you want, and
what do you mean by restoration? If your church is coming
down, repair it, 'restore' it if you will, and get some one who
is practically acquainted with his work; but do not call any
alteration that a fashionable architect, who is paid his five per
cent. for every vagary he may be successful in enabling you to

accept, a 'restoration;' and do not sweep away black old oak
pews that can date back to Queen Anne or George III., and
have a hundred associations, a 'restoration' either, for you will
substitute bald pitch-pine, open benches, stained, and smelling
horribly of varnish." What a boon it would be if some vicar
or rector would put his case fairly when he proposed to restore
his parish church—perhaps a collegiate or abbey one, with
many associations. If he spoke truly, he would in all human
probability address himself to his parishioners in some such
words as these:—" My good friends: Our abbey church is
in a shocking state; for, though it must be admitted that
it is substantial, the weather-stains of centuries deface the
front to the market square. This will be vigorously holy-
stoned down, under the direction of one of the first architects
of the day, who will also add a few pinnacles and crockets, &c.,
in places where the original architect appears not to have seen
that they were needed. Very liberal subscriptions will be
required, for it is almost an honour to get so great a restorer
as the one who is engaged to undertake the work, and he
objects to draw five per cent. on small amounts. The black
oak-work in the chancel will be sand-papered and cleaned with
potash, and the whole edifice turned out like a new one." How
many subscriptions would come in if the appeal were put fairly
as this really is ? On one occasion I heard of a rector who
had coerced an unwilling congregation to get a faculty for " restoring" a parish church of the fourteenth century, and fill the
interior with modern benches in addition. He seemed to prefer
another living, however—perhaps a better one—and left the
congregation to their devices. Right willing they were that
the church of their fathers should remain intact, and even
discharged a liberal legacy he had left them in the shape of

architect's commission; for, if he spared their tabernacle, he did not allow them to escape scot-free. There are instances familiar to some of us where not the vicar or rector, but their better half, was the real restorer. Oak pews, whatever might be their merit artistically, shut out the habiliments and the fair forms of the members of the incumbent's family, and their removal was decreed at the parsonage. Some old farmers remonstrated at the roomy old black oak pews of their ancestors being taken away, and spoke so strongly against the inheritance of their fathers being required of them, that the rector, newly translated from London, began to show evident signs of weakness. He not only did so, but went so far as to express the same at home. He saw no present necessity to carry any point so very distasteful to the feelings of the parishioners, and whatever the views at the rectory might be, the venerable associations of the congregation should be regarded first of all; but his better half, in the interests of his advancing family, soon settled his scruples, and indignantly undertook to manage the thick-witted rustics. "Dost thou now govern the kingdom of Israel? I will give thee the vineyard of Naboth the Jezreelite." Still, it would not be fair to make the clergymen responsible for anything like the ruin which has swept over the land. It is hardly probable that they can, as a rule, have had much occasion to make themselves masters of the principles of building; and seeing that their church stands in need of sundry repairs in parts, they consult some notable restorer, being guided only by the most proper motives, who after long practice has become an adept in managing a well-intentioned rector.

Dorchester is reached soon after passing Clifton Hampden; and it is, indeed, a grand relic of the fourteenth century.

CHANCEL OF DORCHESTER ABBEY.

The restorer here, a rustic said, was "stopped for funds, or else they would have made a worse job of it." At any rate, it has not been excessively altered. There may be a little tinselling under the "Jesse" window, but that is easily removed; and this Jesse window is a great curiosity. It belongs, as the upper part of the lights and the ball flower would show it to be, to the fourteenth century; but it is almost unique. It has been so excellently engraved in "Britton," and in Parker's edition of "Rickman," that it has not been considered necessary to reproduce it here. But it is not the only curious window in this fine building. The Edwardian architect seems to have given full scope to his genius, and revelled in the renovations of the fourteenth century. Perhaps, in no building in England can the revivals of European arts be so conspicuously studied as here; and the designer seemed to have attempted in stone and stained glass that which foreign artists were depicting on canvas. This window seems to be taken from the eleventh chapter of Isaiah: "And there shall come forth a rod out of the stem of Jesse, and a Branch shall grow out of his roots." Jesse is lying down on the sill of the north chancel window, and an imitation of a stem is growing out of him, from which branches spread out to the jambs of the window. There are twenty-five figures on these, nearly all with scrolls, which are held in different attitudes, and originally designed to contain some text or legend. But this is not the only window in the church in which sculpture unusually figures.

Dorchester was formerly the see of a bishop, but the see was removed almost as soon as William I. landed at Hastings. Warton thinks that the present church can boast of no older architecture than that which prevailed in the reign of

Henry III.; but, in the northern wall, he escaped noticing some that dates back to its foundation as a priory in 1140.

The celebrated cross in the churchyard has suffered rather more than the abbey church itself: as a modern expensive head has been added, the ancient one being removed. The details of this head compare rather too closely with the dubious Gothic of a suburban villa, where set stock details are made to do duty for everything. The architecture, however, of old crosses is quite by itself, and requires separate and special study. I have not been able to trace any history belonging to this cross. It seems to have been simply a churchyard cross, and used originally, as such objects were, either as resorts for pilgrims, or for open-air preaching in summer weather, and sometimes as the rendezvous for penitents. Of course, it is an old story how they all suffered in the civil wars; indeed, they excited the principal hatred of Cromwell and his armies, as being the types of Popery. We may think ourselves fortunate in having so many left us; and though these are very various in form—some are canopies, like Chichester and Salisbury; some elegant shafts, like Waltham; and some nearly plain—we may congratulate ourselves upon having the principal forms in use; and Waltham and Northampton will be our examples of the best memorial crosses we shall see

SOUTH AISLE, DORCHESTER CHURCH.

put up in England: and, except as memorials, crosses have, of course, ceased to be erected. The martyrs' memorial, in Oxford, is a really successful copy of the Queen Eleanor Cross at Northampton. Perhaps it is not quite so original, and,

DORCHESTER ABBEY.

indeed, it is not so grand, as the one opposite the Charing Cross Hotel, in London; but that is the very best modern cross that has been erected in England. Still, the Oxford one is really very good, and we should be grateful for it. The same remarks that were made regarding Roman remains, apply equally to crosses; and it is probable that many are lying within a few feet of the surface of the ground; indeed, there are three that I have seen exhumed since this present work was projected. They are in good preservation, and seem to have been buried to preserve them during the stormy period that preceded the reign of Cromwell. One of them is of the age of Henry IV., and two of them date back to some time before the Conquest.

While speaking of memorial crosses, one is apt to think of monuments in churches; and there are some interesting ones in Dorchester, as, indeed, in many other churches around Oxford. From the rude cross-legged knights that we see in the Temple Church, to the elaborate canopied tombs of Elizabeth's time, we may trace many varieties and divergences, and gather not a few hints of the changing habits of the periods. Mr. Bloxham has made some remarks, which so fully coincide with my own observation that I shall borrow them, for I believe they have not been published.

The materials out of which the effigies of the thirteenth century were chiefly sculptured consisted of blocks of dark-coloured marble, destined to be the covers of stone coffins. When ecclesiastics were represented—which they were at this period, always in vestments worn in the performance of the most solemn rites of religion—their heads were often surmounted by elaborate canopies, sculptured horizontally on the slab, with slender shafts on each side of the body, supporting, as it were, the canopy. At the feet of the ecclesiastics of this period a dragon was often represented, in allusion to the verse in the Psalms—"Thou shalt tread upon the lion and adder; the young lion and dragon shalt thou trample under foot." Episcopal effigies are generally represented with a low mitre, holding the pastoral staff in the left hand, whilst the right hand is upheld in the act of benediction.

The sepulchral effigy of a bishop in the Temple Church, London, is of this age, and thus represented. The interesting series of recumbent effigies of abbots in Peterborough Cathedral are represented bare-headed, with the pastoral staff in one hand and a book in the other. But, although a very durable material, this dark-coloured marble was difficult to work, and there was, consequently, a degree of stiffness observable in these marble effigies, which, for the most part, disappeared when the material was of a softer and more pliable nature. There is one sepulchral effigy of an ecclesiastic of this period I should notice, because it is of a singular description. It is the effigy, in dark-coloured marble, of a deacon, holding in one hand a scroll, hanging down, which no doubt was formerly inscribed. It is in the little out-of-the-way church of Avon Dassett, Warwickshire, and is placed under an oxgee-shaped sepulchral arch of at least a century later than the effigy, clearly indicating a rebuilding of the chancel subsequent to the effigy being placed there. But this curious effigy, though nameless, has an historic value : it points to a period when the lower grades of ecclesiastics—deacons, sub-deacons, and even acolytes—were allowed to be presented to churches as incumbents. This practice, once common, was in a great measure put a stop to by a decree of the Council of Lyons. The scroll, hanging down from one of the hands, is found with a few other sepulchral effigies of this period, as with the effigy of a lady at Tilton Church, Leicestershire ; the effigies of a lady and child in Scarcliffe Church, Devonshire ; and the effigy of a lady of the Fitzalan family, in Bedale Church, Yorkshire.

The armed effigies of the early part of the thirteenth century are generally sculptured in marble. Most of the effigies in the Temple Church, London, are of this period. They are distinguishable from the effigies of the fourteenth century, not so much by the details of armour, as by the greater length of the surcoat, and also of the greater length of shield. Armorial bearings now appear on the shield, which is neatly shaped, and fastened to the left arm. The effigies of the ladies are stiffly designed, especially if executed in marble. There is a somewhat gigantic effigy of a lady of this period in Worcester Cathedral. On the whole, then, during the thirteenth century, we may trace a considerable progress in art, both in sculpture and architecture. The patronage of the Crown, tending, no doubt, to foster native talent, was emulated by the nobles and the prelates of the Church; while many of the sepulchral effigies and monuments of this age were sculptured and prepared during the lives of the persons whom they commemorated. This is very evident from the minutiæ of details and the elaborate manner in which many monuments, sculptured in marble, have been executed. The effigy of Bishop Walter de Cantilupe in Worcester Cathedral, which fits the stone coffin in which his remains were, a few years ago, discovered, was evidently executed in his lifetime, and by his order.

But, to return to Dorchester, Skelton says that the bases of ancient crosses have been found in considerable numbers there, thus showing the number of ecclesiastical buildings that belonged to the place at one time; though I fear his reasoning is hardly conclusive, as these were built for very many purposes indeed at one time.

Among the venerable Bishops of Dorchester was Ascwyn, who seemed to have spelt his name in a great variety of ways, and the most pronounceable only is given. His effigy was observed by Leland, but after his time it could not be found, though many attempts were made to discover it. Wood, and Hearne, who was conspicuous for his persistency in ferreting out such things, gave the search up. Accident, however, brought it to light, for, in repairing the pavement in the church, the effigy was discovered, lying horizontally, though it had not the inscription mentioned by Leland.

The dignity of Dorchester, as an episcopal see and a city, seemed to decline with the Saxons, during whose reign it had grown to great importance. But the Danes ravaged all this part of the kingdom; and, assuredly, a rich see like Dorchester would prove too tempting a prize to be resisted. We read of their incursions here in the years 1006, 1009, and the following year. They then made an inroad through the Chiltern Wood, and burnt and plundered Oxford, returning to their country with great spoil. Dorchester was the city that received the first bishop from William the Conqueror. This was Remigino of Feschamp, in Normandy, who was the son of a married priest. It will be remembered, however, that William's army was largely composed of priests. Chroniclers say that Harold's spies reported to him that there were more priests in his adversary's army than he himself had of fighting-men in his own. But the supposed priests were principally good men-at-arms. There were, of course, many priests who were good muscular Christians, but the fact of the upper part of the head being shaven gave the men the appearance of priests; and the same may be noticed in the Bayeux Tapestry.

Dorchester Abbey Church was purchased by Richard Beauforest for £140, and at his death bequeathed by will to the town. "I, Richard Beauforest, of the Towne of

Dorchester, within the County of Oxford, being sicke in bodye, and hole in mynde and memory (thanks be to God), considering nothing is more certen to men than death, and nothing more uncerten than the hour of death, do make my last Wyll and Testamente in form hereafter followinge," &c. &c., and after many bequests quaintly expressed, he says, "Item, I bequeath the Abbey Churche of Dorchester, which I have bought, and the implements thereof, to the Paryshe of Dorchester aforesaid, so that the said parishioners shall not sell, alter, or alienate the saide Churche, Implements, or any part or pell. thereof without the consent of my heirs or executors." Would that similar safeguards were placed round many other venerable buildings that now are so sadly disfigured and changed from their old lineaments.

The ancient bridge was taken down in 1815; but it must have been a very picturesque structure, and it dated back to the reign of Edward III.

Dorchester has been called Hydropolis, or water town, the first syllable of its name, Dor, being doubtless akin to *dwr*, the Welsh word for water; and Leland speaks of it under that designation. It stands almost at the confluence of the Thames and Thame; and, as the upper waters of the Thames have been often called the Isis, it has sometimes been said that the junction of these two streams forms the great metropolitan river. But this is a mistake; the Thames is the Thames from its source in Gloucestershire to its termination at the Nore. The guidebooks mention that at the junction of the four roads between Dorchester and Balden was the original "Golden Cross" inn, where the notable Jonathan Bradford resided, who was tried for the murder of Mr. Hayes, and who was condemned and executed, justly as it turned out, though he was not the actual

perpetrator of the deed. He went into his chamber for the
purpose of murdering him ; but he was too late—the servant
of the victim had forestalled him. This the servant himself
confessed on his death-bed, some eighteen months after.

But all Dorchester is full of interest, and it has played a
conspicuous part in history from the time that it was a centre
of Roman civilisation to the time when it became the largest
bishopric in England.

Steventon is in the hundred of Ock, and is about four miles
to the south of Abingdon. The direct road lies through
Drayton, where all the houses and cottages have pleasant
gardens ; but doubtless the most picturesque road lies through
Sutton Courtney and Milton, and past the water-mills elsewhere
alluded to. Here there was at one time an alien priory,
as it was called, of black monks, which was a cell of Béc Harle-
win in Normandy, and the manor was granted by Henry I.
to the foundation ; but in the wars between Edward III. and
France this manor found new owners. He fancied that by
the simplest interpretation of the Salique law he should be
King of France, and after disposing of Isabella and Mortimer,
he suppressed all the alien houses in England. The manor of
Steventon was conveyed to John, Bishop of Salisbury, and
Roger Walden, who are supposed to have been trustees of
certain crown properties, though there is some obscurity about
the transaction. It had previously been sold to Sir Hugh
Calveley, who had followed Edward through his wars, and
it would appear to have been in his possession for only a
short time ; indeed, he had not made it a residence, and
perhaps parted with it on easy conditions. It is almost
tempting here to mention how a study like this will
enhance the value of many a familiar object, quite accepting

the risk of a charge of unjustifiable ignorance. Within a few miles of where this is written is a fine old parish church, pleasantly situated near Beeston Castle, which was rendered

PERCY ROBERTS Sc.

SUTTON COURTNEY MILL-POOL.

conspicuous by the gallant stand it made in the civil wars; and whether we may think the side the defenders were contending for was the right one or the wrong one, the time has long gone by for withholding our admiration and sympathy for

their devotion. A skull is shown in a small museum on
Chester walls with a couple of swan-shot embedded in it during
an assault at Beeston, in Cromwell's time. The owner of

STEVENTON CAUSEWAY.

it lived, it is said, for many years after; but the ancient
keeper of the museum cannot tell which side he was fighting
on; he fancies—safely, one would think—that he was a Round-
head. Close by the ruins of Beeston Castle, and within sight,

on a clear day, of Chester, is Bunbury Church. It is a quiet
country parish church of some architectural pretensions, and
it has a very noble west window of the fourteenth century
style. There are several remains about it that show it must
have been a place of importance at one time, and some of its
remains connect it with the collegiate establishment that was
founded at the termination of the French wars. How very
often we may pass by records that we have seen time after
time, and not know the great historic interest that belongs to
them.

Again and again I have extended a summer's walk to
Bunbury, and seen the effigy of Sir Hugh Calveley in the
chancel, but only learned since writing the present chapters
that he had ever taken any conspicuous part in history; but
he had been with Edward III. in the French wars, and assisted
in the lesson that, as has been said, was to be taught the
world at Cressy—a lesson the English themselves learned at
Bannockburn. The old social and political fabric of the Middle
Ages rested on a military base, and that base was suddenly
withdrawn. "The Church had struck down the noble, the
bondsman proved more than a match for the knight in sheer
hard fighting, and from the day of Cressy feudalism tottered
slowly but surely to its grave."

The monument of Sir Hugh Calveley is of alabaster, and
situated in the middle of the chancel of Bunbury Church.
It is a large altar-tomb, elaborately adorned with Gothic
niches, and shields, and armorial bearings. Sir Hugh, who
is of gigantic proportions, but finely chiselled, lies down at full
length on the top, with his hands closed over his breast. He
is dressed in plate armour, richly ornamented down the seams,
with gorget and skirt of mail. There is a lion at his feet, as is

so usual in monuments of this period, and his head rests on a calve's head issuing from a ducal coronet. Sir Hugh does not appear, however, to have distinguished himself until the treaty of Bretigny, when France was described by Petrarch as a vast wilderness, roads overgrown with weeds, towns quite deserted, and even Paris left a solitude.

The finding such associations as these between Oxford and Cheshire, is surely a strong incentive to linger round familiar objects, and read their history. Sir Hugh founded the very formidable army of veterans, called "The Companions," and they were responsible for many of the outrages that devastated the lands of France. They held themselves free to join any expedition or do any mischief, where plunder might crown their prowess. They are chiefly celebrated for the part they took in the wars of John de Montford, who claimed the crown of Brittany; and they fought at the battle of Auray, in 1364. This battle was decisive, and was won principally by the prowess of Sir John Chandos and Sir Hugh Calveley. There is a commonly-received tradition that Sir Hugh was one of the thirty champions who fought a similar number of Bretons. This body of companions in arms assisted greatly in expelling Peter the Cruel from the Spanish throne; but when the Black Prince espoused the cause of the dethroned monarch, they arranged themselves again under his standard, and, for some time, reinstated him in his misgoverned dominions. The victory of Najara, again, is said to be due to the gallant knights of Auray. Sir Hugh is said to have married a princess of Arragon; but Lysons says that, in conning over the list, these princesses can all be accounted for in other ways of distribution.

From the possession of Sir Hugh Calveley, as has been said,

Steventon passed to the crown, and now the living is in the gift of the Dean and Chapter of Westminster. Dugdale only slightly mentions the alien priory that was suppressed here; indeed, his principal chronicles are those which existed at the time of the Reformation. The Abbey of Bec was a great institution, and could boast of no less a man than Anselm as its head. "A walk through Normandy," a recent English writer has said, "teaches one more of the age of our history than all the books in the world. The whole story of the Conquest stands written on the stately vault of the minster at Caen, which still covers the tomb of the Conqueror. The name of each hamlet by the roadside has its memories for English ears; a fragment of castle wall marks the home of the Bruce; a tiny little village preserves the name of Percy. The very look of the country and its people seems familiar to us: the peasant, in his cap and blouse, recalls the features and build of the small English farmer; the fields about Caen, with their dense hedgerows, their elms, their apple-orchards, are the very picture of an English country-side. On the windy heights around rise the square grey keeps which Normandy handed on to the cliffs of Richmond or the banks of the Thames; while huge cathedrals lift themselves over the red-tiled roofs of little market towns—the models of the stately fabrics which superseded the lowlier churches of Dunstan."

This Anselm was removed from Bec to Canterbury, and became one of the greatest, if not the greatest bishop that ever graced an English see; and may be said almost to have altered, and that very much for the better, the whole tone of the religious houses.

Roman coins are found in great abundance near Dorchester;

and these are mostly of the lower empire, and some are of Carausius, who reigned in Britain. It is said there are many coins yet buried in fields in the neighbourhood. A very interesting altar was also discovered here, and removed to Broom Park, in Kent.

Skelton says—" The only military work now to be seen in Dorchester is that called the Dyke Hills." Several writers have supposed these banks to be of Roman creation, while others are of a contrary opinion. They were, perhaps, thrown up to command the passages of the two rivers. As the extremities of the banks join the river, from which a sufficient supply of water might be occasionally turned into the trench between the banks, by this means the passages of the Thame and Isis might be commanded; or, as Dr. Plot conjectures, they may have been part of the outworks of the fortifications, the bold remains of which yet present themselves on Long Wittenham Hill, Berks, which is on the opposite side of the river. The Dyke Hill banks closely resemble those called Grims-dyke, between Unffield and Newnham, near Wallingford, pointing over the Thames to Chosely, Berks—so closely, indeed, that they seem to have been raised by the same people. And if Grimsdyke, which is not more than five Roman miles from it, be of Roman erection, one may confidently pronounce the same of the Dyke Hills at Dorchester.

If, in place of the Dorchester road, we turn to the south, after leaving Abingdon, we shall still find abundant scenes of interest and beauty. The road, it is true, for some way, is through poor and half-cultivated land, often not even enclosed, and many of the cottagers seem to have advanced but little in material prosperity or education since the time when Oxford University was first founded; but we soon emerge from the waste; and, whether we take the Sutton Wick or Sutton Courtney road, we shall soon find ourselves in scenes of beauty; and if we proceed farther along in the same direction, we shall

CHANCEL OF MILTON CHURCH.

enter a country that has yet to be almost explored, so many antiquarian relics does it contain. This road joins the Ridge-way that crosses over the summit of the Berkshire Hills, and reminds one of the more celebrated Boxmore-way. The Ridge is a grand specimen of Roman engineering, and it is frequently called Ickleton Street, which was its ancient name.

Milton Church has been somewhat needlessly restored in parts, though the old inhabitants say it was in excellent order before the restorer came. The only fault that could be found with its durable stone, they said, was that it had got dark-looking; and if the untouched windows may be taken as any criterion, it is pretty sure that the money spent might have been more usefully employed. The chancel of this church is excellently well proportioned, and the segmental-headed windows are somewhat unusual in the Decorated style, to which it belongs; still they are not unique, for some even perfectly flat window-heads of the fourteenth century will occur to every one who has taken an interest in country churches. The chancel of this church, like Bicester and others in the neighbourhood of Oxford, is higher than the nave, and this is, many will say, a great improvement. The common form of an English church—namely, a spire at the west end, a nave and a chancel each descending by steps—is, as Mr. Petit has pointed out, almost fatal to picturesqueness. It has to be combined with surroundings to alter its natural shape and to give it a new sky-line.

There are great numbers of water-mills in this neighbour-hood; as many, indeed, as would astonish any one from the northern counties, where they are not common. Perhaps they are not quite so picturesque always as the Welsh mills. The mountainous country there admits of a much greater fall of water, and hence we get the overshot wheels, which are not only more powerful, but are generally contrived with greater variety of form than the undershot ones; some of the latter are, however, very rural and pleasant.

Milton Mill, which is here shown, is about three-quarters
of a mile from the church, and is reached by a beautifully-
shaded walk that skirts Milton Hall Park. The buildings,
though partly of wood, are sufficiently substantial, and the

MILTON MILL.

nook in which it is situated is a very picture of rural retirement and delight.   The same stream that turns this mill turns
three others within the space of a mile, and another is shown
between this one and Sutton Courtney. An artist might go very
far indeed before he found any subject more thoroughly cut out
for his pencil.   A third one would have been shown, but the

miller had run his dam off, and unshipped his wheel, so as to deepen the water and increase the power of his machinery. His remarks on water-power showed that he had spent an advanced life in making useful observations. There are numbers of fish in this brook, and in the clear abundant water that runs past Milton Hall we should expect to find

STEVENTON MILL.

trout; but, though I have often approached the banks quietly, it never fell to my lot to see any. Dace, perch, and gudgeon seem to be the principal denizens. Angling books say that the Thames near Oxford abounds with fine trout, but fishermen tell a somewhat different tale. A few may be taken in the course of a year, but the capture of one is generally chronicled in the London papers, and it will probably be followed by many letters regarding Thames trout, and the probability or

otherwise of their being a separate species. Trout are sometimes found in strange places. I was passing by a length of
canal in Cheshire which had been drawn off for cleaning, and
among other fish a fine trout was captured; it must have
measured a foot in length; and was in excellent condition, yet
the junction of the canal with the River Dee, from which it
draws its supply of water, is thirty miles. If, however, the
bass alluded to have any kind of fair play till they can hold
their own, there will be no want of excellent fish at Milton
Mill and in all the streams that are near it. The one between
Milton and Sutton Courtney is, perhaps, still more picturesque
than Milton Mill. A flat spans the brook, and one is reminded of Sir Walter Scott's description of a rivulet, if we
compare this one in July with the same in November :—

> " Late gazing down the steepy lynn
> That hems our little garden in,
> Low in its dark and narrow glen
> You scarce the rivulet might ken,
> So thick the tangled greenwood grew,
> So feeble trilled the streamlet through ;
> Now murmuring hoarse, and frequent seen
> Through bush and briar, no longer green,
> An angry brook it sweeps the glade,
> Brawls over rock and wild cascade,
> And foaming down with doubled speed,
> Hurries its waters to the Tweed."

The different levels of roof, and the clinker-boarding mingled
with the stonework, lend a great charm to this quaint old
building.

How the use these little rills are put to must often remind
a passer-by of the enormous water-power that is wasted annually,
or, indeed, hourly, in our island ! It has been calculated that
the River Dee alone, if the tidal forces that sweep up its

estuary are included, would supply power for every manufactory in England, and then there would be plenty to spare.
The coals that blacken the atmosphere might be saved for
grates or engines, and all the land would be better and richer.
Not that the Dee is mentioned beyond any other river, for
its course from Bala Lake to Chester is only thirty miles, and
it is neither broad nor deep; but it may serve to illustrate the
wanton waste of power that prevails over the land, and contrast
the saving industry of these millers that can turn the tiny
streams round Oxford to such good account. The Dee has a
vast natural dam in Bala Lake, which is so constructed that a
pair of gates, and little else, would place millions of tons of
water-power under control; and it was once proposed to supply
Liverpool with water from this source, and control the flow, so
that it should not be a furious river one day and a large brook
another. One advantage promised by the promoters was a vast
increase in the salmon supply, and indeed in the trout-fishing
also.

CHAPTER V.

" Nimium ne crede colori."

Walk from Oxford to Godstow—Laying Foundation-stone of Godstow Nunnery—Rosamond—Ruins of Godstow—Catherine Buckley—Storm of 1703—Henry II. and his general Character—Clifford Castle—Road of Islip, and Suburban Architecture round Oxford—Cherwell Bridge—Edward the Confessor.

THE walk from Oxford to Godstow, along the banks of the Thames, is absolutely delightful; two miles, the guide-books call it, though it is somewhat more. The breezes that follow the current of the Thames give it some slight feeling of coolness on the hottest summer's day; and there are many pleasant, peaceful homes away from the river's bank. The guide-books say that there is good angling here, and, they truly say, there is an excellent inn close by. Adjacent to Godstow is the village of Wolvercott, where the University Press Mill is situated, and where, according to Holinshed, King Memphric of the Britons was seized in a dingle by wolves, and devoured. He was traditionally regarded as the first founder of Oxford.

John of St. John, lord of Wolvercote and Stanton, gave the site for this nunnery, which was consecrated in the year 1138, and it was dedicated to St. John, out of compliment to its founder. It seems to have been quite a favourite house, even from its commencement, and King Stephen and his wife were present, and endowed it; many other bishops and nobles were also at the laying of the foundation-stone, and they gave liberally towards its revenues. The modern style of laying

THE THAMES, NEAR GODSTOW.

foundation-stones was observed even then : a banquet, complimentary addresses to each other, and a collection well organised beforehand. Albericus, the Bishop of Hostia, happened to be in England at the time, and he was quite equal to the occasion. He was the Pope's legate, and had no difficulty in finding means to quicken the piety of the subscribers. He proclaimed a release of one year from all enforced penances to all who contributed with sufficient liberality to its resources ; and the very extensive lands that were conveyed to it on this occasion and subsequently were confirmed by charter in the reigns of King Stephen and Richard I.

Godstow is principally known to modern history as being the residence of Rosamond Clifford—the " Fair Rosamond," as she has generally been called. This lady was the daughter of Walter, Lord Clifford, of Clifford Castle, in Herefordshire, and she is described as having been endowed with a lively wit, and, of course, as possessing exquisite beauty. According to Grose, the labyrinth where she was a resident consisted of arches and winding walls of stone, " into whose recesses it was impossible for any stranger to penetrate ; " and there she lived for several years. She was the mother of William Longland, Earl of Salisbury ; and Geoffry, Bishop of Lincoln.

Some pages of English history have been filled up with accounts of Fair Rosamond and her bower ; and she has excited as much attention as if she had really occupied some prominent place in English history, and founded a dynasty. The tales of the " ball of silk," and the " jealous Queen Eleanor," are, of course, fabrications ; as the engineering difficulties that any one who might feel disposed to try the experiment would find in the way of such a story would prove. The old story, of course, goes that the energetic queen discovered a ball of silk—

a green one, the careful chroniclers relate—at the entrance of the bower, and the beauty shrank from observation. She had hold of either the loose end or the ball, and fled to her hiding-place, hotly pursued by Queen Eleanor of Poitou and Guienne, who was quite dazzled by Rosamond's beauty when she arrived at the sanctum; but, on recovering her self-possession, she presented Rosamond with the cup of poison—that had not been spilled in the exciting chase—and so closed her career. Other accounts say that the secret of the entrance to the bower was forced from a knight who had charge of the lady during the absence of the king in the French wars. A chalice, or some such figure, on her tomb probably gave rise to the tale of the poison, for it is a matter of history that Rosamond died a natural death.

During her residence at Woodstock, she made several visits to Godstow, and tradition says that she was lectured, and taken very generally to task, by the superiors of the nunnery; but she replied that she was perfectly satisfied, and time would show how innocent she was of any wrong, and told them that she was sure, in confirmation of her words, a certain tree she mentioned would turn into stone, as a proof that she was with the saints in heaven. Of course, the fossilisation took place; and, at the time of the dissolution of monasteries, a fossil trunk was shown as being the actual one that attested her pious life.

The ruins of Godstow have diminished very much indeed in modern times. In Grose's work there is an engraving of the building—which figures here, though it was more complete then—and also of a large church-tower which belonged to the nunnery. The buildings showed that it must at one time have been very considerable. The sketch from which the engraving was taken was made, we are informed, in 1761; but now the tower is gone, and the only remains are those shown in the small engraving at the end of the chapter. In the chapel, or the ruins of it which were still standing when Grose wrote, was the coffin which contained the remains of Rosamond; but it was made in two compartments, with a stone division down the middle.

There is one curious feature in the ruins of Godstow which is not common in ancient buildings, but which has been noticed in earlier descriptions of the nunnery: the walls have been stuccoed—"plastered" Grose calls them, in his work written during the last century.

Of course, the old tradition of underground passages is rife here. It pertains to every religious establishment of respectability; and, if the accredited subterranean passages of some counties could be put in blue lines on an Ordnance map, the localities would be fairly well drained for agricultural purposes. A labouring man told Mr. Hanwell, who was the treasurer of Christ Church College, that he had seen an underground passage at Godstow which, he was told, led to Woodstock, and travelled through part of it. He passed three gateways, and then gave it up. Of course, if there is any truth in the story at all, it must have been some unused drain, for the passage from there to Woodstock could not have been less than six miles. One thing is clear: it can hardly have been through that where the memorable skein of green silk was unravelled.

Catherine Buckley was the last Abbess of Godstow, and she seems to have been an estimable lady. Again and again she besought the king to spare the revenues of the establishment; but they were too large to be passed by, though she

was supported in her petitions by many gentlemen who lived
in the county, and whose daughters were pupils and boarders
at the convent. They urged that nothing could be brought
against the establishment, and perhaps truly said that the
way of life of the inmates was free from reproach; but all
to no effect. The fiat had gone forth, and Godstow was
disestablished, and the abbess and sixteen nuns were
pensioned.

In the year 1703 a furious storm swept down a large
walnut-tree, and exposed an ancient tombstone, round which
its roots had twined, and on it was the legend, " Godestowe une
Chauntrie F." Grose says that this was the subject of much
argument and conjecture, and tells us where we may find the
speculations ; but these, indeed, take us back to a period in
antiquarian research when anything was made out of anything.
The reality of the exposure of the slab is somewhat confirmed
by the circumstance that a storm of exceeding violence swept
over England in 1703 ; and it is always pleasant to find unexpected and unconcerted testimony. The battle of Clontarf—
which is said to have been won, or lost, as it may be regarded,
under peculiar circumstances of the tide—has been the subject
of scientific inquiry, and the astronomers precisely confirm the
conditions of the ebb and flow of high water that the chroniclers
have narrated to have happened. Now it may be remembered
that when the Duke of Marlborough was in the height of his
power, many poets were commissioned to write his praises ;
but their productions are now little known. Addison, however,
who was in great penury at the time, was commissioned to
invoke the muses by the Chancellor of the Exchequer, who had
been deputed by the Lord Treasurer to do so, and he produced
a poem that has apparently escaped oblivion. His theme is

the Duke calm and firm in all the din of battle, and he thus alludes to him in one part of the piece :—

> "So when an angel by divine command,
>   With rising tempests shakes a guilty land,
>   Such as of late o'er pale Britannia passed ;
>   Calm and serene he drives the furious blast,
>   And, pleased the Almighty's orders to perform,
>   Rides in the whirlwind, and directs the storm."

Macaulay was the first to see the real meaning of this passage, and he refers it to some great tempest that must have been the common theme at the time, and his interpretation is confirmed by records of there having been such a storm in November, 1703; no doubt this is the same hurricane that uprooted the walnut-tree at Godstow.

There are not many particulars about Rosamond, though Delany celebrates her beauty in a lengthy ballad, in which he says :—

> "Her crispèd locks like threads of golde
>   Appeared to all men's sight ;
>   Her sparkling eyes, like Orient pearles,
>   Did cast a heavenly lighte."

We have authentic records, however, of the appearance of Henry II., and it is thus sketched by a great historian of the present day :—"His practical, serviceable frame suited the hardest worker of his time. There was something in his very build and look—in the square, stout frame, the fiery face, the close-cropped hair, the prominent eyes, the bull-neck, the coarse, strong hands, the bowed legs—that marked out the keen, stirring, coarse-fibred man of business. 'He never sits down,' says one who observed him closely ; 'he is always on his legs, from morning till night.' Orderly in business,

careless in appearance, sparing in diet, never resting or giving
his servants rest, chatty, inquisitive, endowed with a singular
charm of address and strength of memory, obstinate in love
and hatred, a fair scholar, a great hunter, his general air that
of a rough, busy man, Henry's personal character told directly
on the character of his reign." We have not any such record
of Rosamond, and all descriptions of her beauty are conjectural.
It may have been very great—probably it was; but Henry may
have been captivated by other qualities, or his estimate of
beauty may have differed very far from our own.

The old tale of the Bishop of Lincoln going to Godstow,
and finding a tomb, with candles and drapery, and choristers,
and everything, in fact, belonging to a departed saint, has
probably truth on its side; and it is quite likely that, "in pious
anger and holy grief, he solemnly cursed the rascally thief."
Certainly the altar-tomb had to be removed, though the nuns
in residence took a kindlier view of the matter, and still
preserved the remains with care and affection.

The road to Islip is almost due north from Oxford, and,
after leaving the city limits, it is remarkably pleasant. For
some way outside the liberties, there are lines of detached
villas, built in brick and stone, and much architectural care
and skill have been expended upon them. Many of them are
of considerable dimensions, and surrounded with neatly-kept
gardens and glass-houses. One feels quite pleased to see so
much variety of design, and to contrast it with the careless
architecture that so often prevails in suburban villas. Yet,
for all that, the general effect is hardly pleasing. There is
a want of repose; and this want of repose is exactly the
stumbling-block of modern villa architects. It is not, of course,
necessary that a front should be flat to give it repose; it may

want it, in spite of that—just as a landscape may want breadth, even if as large as a dining-room wall, and yet may possess that inestimable quality, if only a couple of inches square. The few Oxford gables that have been engraved in these chapters are conducive to repose in a structure; not that they are tame, or flat—quite, indeed, the reverse: they are as full of angles and returns as any of the villas we are now considering—but they have a certain amount of vigour and character, all so evidently unstudied, that, if one of them is in a front, it blends and harmonises minor details. And, until modern designers study the picturesque effect of their works as they will appear when erected, they may study Palladio or Rickman or Britton in vain.

Low, indeed, as art had sunk in the Georgian age, the feeling for picturesqueness and appropriateness was not quite stamped out; and often in a Romanesque house, with its wreaths and broken pediments, and stone quoins, in the earlier Georgian period, we can detect some unstudied and unconscious artistic taste: at any rate, we may be nearly sure that it will, to a great extent, adapt itself to its surroundings. There is, indeed, a way in which apparent wealth of space can be given to a building that has, in reality, none to spare—as we do not need to pass the Oxford colleges themselves to learn; and yet there may be a sort of fussiness about even a large building, that quite diminishes its proportions—as, indeed, it would not be very difficult to exemplify in some modern and costly mansions.

It would seem as if, in all styles of architecture, whether old or new, some established principles always kept rising to the surface, to fill the requirements of the time; and the works of an acknowledged man—such as Vanbrugh, or Adams, or Inigo

Jones—however foreign they may seem to our modern ideas, have always some value about them. It would be a long list to fill up of the able architects that, from Henry II.'s time to the present day, have adorned England with shapely buildings. But they did succeed each other in proper course; and, whether they knew it or not, their genius reflected from one to the other. It was all in vain that Wren used to call the architects of cathedrals, and abbey churches, and monastic piles, "Goths." The word was used in derision at first; and this really great man fancied that, by applying it to the architecture of all the monkish ages, it could be reduced to contumely. The Goths and the Vandals had overrun the city which is called eternal, and the treasures they overturned would doubtless be enough to astonish us, and enlighten us as to many forms of architecture that, in our simple reception of the classic orders—Doric, Ionic, and Corinthian—we have so long considered as final. But Wren himself adapted the construction of Gothic buildings in his very best works.

The road to Islip is through a rich agricultural country, and, a short way before we reach the village, we cross a bridge over the Cherwell—a massive, well-built stone structure, as, indeed, all the bridges round Oxford are. One is tempted to linger on it, and look over the parapet into the shallow waters below, and watch the great numbers of fresh-water fish that seem to regard it as a resting-place. When I have passed over, there have been shoals of dace and roach, and some carp of considerable weight. At first it is noticeable that, under such circumstances—as soon, that is, as a head appears over a bridge—there is a general stampede; but after a little time, if it is apparent that you mean no harm, a truce is struck up, and the fishes soon resume their former shallows. This is true

of all animated nature; and I lately saw, on a private lake
attached to a dwelling, at least a thousand wild ducks and
geese that never left the water. They laid eggs and hatched
young ones within sight of the house; and yet I was assured
that, outside the proscribed limits, they were as wild as any
ducks or geese in the British Isles. So tame were they, however, in their refuge in Dorsetshire, that one morning, in
walking along the lake, a wild goose suddenly appeared, in a
menacing attitude, fearing I should disturb her young. There
were no less than ten different species of ducks on the lake
—from pin-tails and poachards to the common wild duck—
but all were equally tame. I was assured, however—though,
indeed, it needed no assurance—that three minutes' shooting
would have emptied the pool, though it was probably two miles
in circumference, and the birds would have joined their fellows.

This digression is only to illustrate what was started with:
that if you let any wild thing know you are not a foe, it soon
becomes tame.

Below the Cherwell Bridge is a deep pool, suggestive of
heavy pike and perch. Probably there is no water so near
Oxford where a good basket of fish could be made more readily.

Islip, according to Camden, is a mean, ill-built village. It
gave birth to Edward the Confessor, whose father had a palace
here, which stood on the north side of the church; and the
chapel thereof served as a barn, but was taken down and
rebuilt a few years ago, so there are no traces of the original
edifice.

William de Curtlyngton, Abbot of Westminster (1315–33),
built the manor-house anew, very handsomely, and in a different
place. "The font, in which the Confessor was supposed to have
been baptised, was long used at the 'Plume of Feathers' inn

for a washing-basin, till bought by Mr. Brown, of Nether
Kiddington, where it stands in the garden of Lady Mostyn,
daughter and heir of the late Sir George Brown, Bart., on a
handsome pedestal, with some lines rather pious than learned."
The font where he was christened has been removed several
times, and I have not had the good fortune to see it; but
some doubts have been raised, it would seem, as to whether it
is not of somewhat later style than might be expected from its
history.   The style of architecture would, however, readily
show; he lived at the same time as the Conqueror; and there
are not a few fonts of the same period in existence in some
country churches.

A halo of tenderness, as has been well said, hangs round
the memory of the last king of the old English stock, and
legends are told of his pious life and gentle, blithe manners.
He gained for himself, indeed, the name of "the Confessor,"
and was enshrined as a saint at Westminster.   "He was the
one figure that stood out bright against the darkness, when
England lay trodden under the foot by Norman conquerors,
and so dear became his memory that liberty and independence
itself seemed incarnate in his name."   "There is something
shadow-like," Dr. Green says, "in his thin form, the delicate
complexion, the transparent womanly hands, that contrasted
with the blue eyes and golden hair of his race; and it is almost
as a shadow that he glides over the political stage.   The work
of government was done by sterner hands."

Some time since the *Builder* contained an interesting notice
of the discovery of Edward's coffin, which had not, perhaps,
been published before.   It is extracted from the accounts of
the Paymaster of Works and Buildings belonging to the Crown
during the reign of James II. :—

THE MARKET ELM, ISLIP.

" Paid to Master Banks for a large coffin by him made to enclose the body of St. Edward the Confessor, and setting it up in its place in the year 1685, £6 2s. 8d., and to William Backe, locksmith, for large hinges and rivetts, and 2 crossebarrs for said coffin, £2 17s. 7d." Keepe, writing in 1681, or four years before this, says, " I have seen a large chest or coffin, bound about with strong bands of iron, lying about the midst of the inside of this shrine, where, I suppose, the body of the pious Confessor may still be conserved." Four years after this time, at the taking down of the scaffolding that had been erected for the coronation of James II., a hole was broken in the lid of the coffin, and Keepe put his hand into it, and, he says, " Turning the bones which I felt there, I drew from underneath the shoulder-bones a crucifix, richly adorned and enamelled, and a gold chain twenty-four inches in length." These relics were accepted by James, and, as has been said, the chain and the crucifix of the last of the line of Saxon kings, were used by the last of the Stuarts. But there are several walls and buildings in Islip that denote antiquity; the stones of some of the barns and farm buildings are so neatly squared and even yet so very " plumb," that there is no difficulty in referring them to some pious foundation of early days.

The present rectory-house was built by Bishop South, who was the rector here about two hundred years ago, and it is an admirable specimen of the building of the period. Formerly, Islip was the country seat of the Deans of West-minster; but this ceased to be when pluralities were abolished. Dean Buckland, who held the living, was the last that enjoyed it in addition to his deanery. Of course, this readily accounts for the number of eminent men who are connected with Islip. Perhaps few are better known than the witty Bishop South, of whom so many good tales are told. On one occasion, it is said that he was preaching before King Charles II., and observed the monarch fast asleep in his seat, when he suddenly stopped, and called, "Lord Lauderdale!" in a loud tone of voice, and when the amazed nobleman stood up, the Bishop politely requested him not to snore so heavily, for fear of waking his Majesty.

Bishop South was the son of an eminent London merchant, and was born at Hackney, in Middlesex, in 1633. He was educated by Dr. Busby at Westminster School, and elected to Christ Church, Oxford, in 1651, receiving ordination from one of the deprived Bishops in 1658.

The next year he preached an assize sermon before the judges, and made a violent attack upon the Independents, which ingratiated him with the Presbyterians, who, however, in their turn came in for a full share of his satire. He was made domestic chaplain to Lord Clarendon, and taken under his protection during a stormy period of English history. The graceful address he made on the occasion of Lord Clarendon's election to the Chancellorship of Oxford pleased the great statesman, and paved the way to South's future fortunes. Few men more fully understood than he how to make friends with the powers that be. Of this he gave an excellent example when, in 1681, he preached a sermon before Charles II. on the subject of the unexpected turns of fortune in human life, and took for his text Proverbs xvi., 33rd verse, and exemplified the fact by the instances of Agathocles and Masaniello, and after quoting several verses from the same Book, and saying that the throne of a king is established by righteousness, and that pride goeth before destruction, and a haughty spirit before a fall, he suddenly astonished his hearers by breaking out upon Cromwell in the language that is credibly recorded : "And who that beheld such a beggarly bankrupt as that fellow Cromwell, first entering the parliament-house with a threadbare torn cloak and greasy hat—perhaps neither of them paid for—could have suspected that in the space of so few years he should, by the murder of one king, and the banishment of another, ascend the throne?" Charles was delighted, and broke out in laughter, saying at the same time, "Tell me, Rochester, when there is a vacant bishopric."

John Ireland, another rector, was born at Ashburton, in Devonshire, in 1761. His father was a butcher in that town, and Gifford, the translator of Juvenal, was his fellow-student. He matriculated at Oxford as Bible Clerk of Oriel College, and on taking the degree of B.A. he was appointed to a curacy in the neighbourhood of Ashburton. In 1793 he became vicar of Croydon, and he held the living for twenty-three years, and in 1802 he was promoted to a prebendal stall at Westminster. On the death of his friend, Dr. Vincent, he became rector of Islip. He was the author of the celebrated five discourses, containing certain arguments for and against the reception of Christianity by the ancient Jews and Greeks—his *Nuptiæ Sacræ*, &c., &c.; but he is best known as one of the early contributors to the *Quarterly*, in conjunction with his friend Canning, and his early school-fellow at Ashburton, W. Gifford.

The career of the latter was even more remarkable than his own. He was a desolate orphan at thirteen, and a cabin-boy in a coasting schooner till he was fifteen years old, when he became apprenticed for seven years to a shoe-maker. During his apprenticeship he was an eager reader, and

procured books wherever he could.   A surgeon happened to
notice his devotion to literature, and took an interest in him.
He soon released him from his articles, and placed him first
at school, and then at Exeter College, Oxford.   He met
with an influential friend in Earl Grosvenor, who gave him
the charge of his son, Lord Belgrave, with whom he travelled
on the Continent.   He ultimately became editor of the
Quarterly, at a salary of £900 a year.

GODSTOW NUNNERY.

CHAPTER VI.

"It was an ancient, venerable hall,
And once surrounded by a moat and wall;
A part was added by a squire of taste."—*Crabbe.*

Town of Bicester—Priory—Prior Wantyng—Seat of Blount Family after Dissolution—
Priory Estates—Stanley Family—George Stanley and Richard III.—Glynnes
purchase Ambrosden—Bicester Church—Bicester Dovecote and Pigeons—Eynsham—
American Weed—University Paper-mill—Ink of Oxford MSS.

GABLE AT ST. ALDATE'S.

BICESTER is a very pleasant, old-fashioned
town, situated some thirteen miles from
Oxford; and there are names about its site
redolent of old English associations. One
part is called Market End, and the other
King's End. In Shrimpton's carefully
compiled guide to the neighbourhood of
Oxford a number of possible derivations
of the name are suggested, and the authorities are accurately given; but to the
general reader such matters have little
interest, and often the archæological re-
search that has been expended over guide-books is like pearls
thrown away. Whether baron or abbot of historic name
granted manors to any religious foundation is generally a
matter to be skipped over, so long as the ruins are of themselves pleasing; unless, indeed, we happen to represent the
line of the favoured one who received the lands of the monastery

at the Dissolution, when even the dreariest details of boundary become intensely interesting.

The history of Bicester Priory, however, is very curious. It was founded by Gilbert Basset, in 1182, in the twenty-eighth year of the reign of Henry II., when so great an impetus had been given to the building and endowing religious houses by the influence of Becket and the king. It was intended for a prior and eleven canons, in imitation of Christ and His eleven disciples; and Basset's wife, who survived him, contributed still further to its endowment.

The rules of the Augustines, by which body it was held, were among the simplest and best of all orders. Among others, it was required that no man should call anything his own, but everything was to be common, and the rich were to respect the poor. No one was to be admitted to a monastery without trial; and when he left he was to carry nothing away with him.

There is a curious instance of how rigidly they adhered to their rules in the instance of John Wantyng, the prior. He held his office for fourteen years, but certainly made no profit out of it; for when he wished to resign, through age and infirmity, the following provision was made:—

Translation.—" John Wantyng, prior of Burcester, not having from any other quarter the substance of this world, from whence he is able to support himself according to his proper state, rank, and age, hath resigned the said priory; the bishop hath preferred to the same priory Edmund Wycomb, and assigns to the said John for his maintenance a place called the *trymles*, situated within the priory aforesaid, with its garden; also, the said John shall have for the term of his life, for the clothing and stipend of his servant, five marks;

also, he shall have four carts-load of firewood from the wood or coppice of the said prior, and as much bread and beer, fish and flesh, and other eatables and drinkables, as two canons of the said priory have been accustomed to receive. He shall have, also, every month, two pounds of wax candles for his chamber; and shall have also every week twelve flagons of beer, and thirty-three conventual loaves for himself and servants."

The priory buildings remained for some time after the dissolution in 1536. The refectory, the bursary, the chapter-house, the locutory, and the dormitory must have occupied a large space of ground; and they were afterwards converted into a mansion for the Blount family.

BICESTER PRIORY.

All that now remains is the small farmhouse shown here. It is about forty feet in length, and forms part of the boundary wall belonging to the monastery. It is supposed to have been a lodge for the accommodation of travellers. A well of never-failing water in the garden was the object of high veneration, and resorted to by pilgrims from great distances. This well was for long unused, and became choked up, till in the dry summer of 1666, the year of the Great Fire, Mr. Colset, the lord of the manor, cleared the weeds and *débris*, when this was followed by a great gush of water, which not a few of the people believed to be a miracle wrought by St. Edburg. The "History of Bicester" says:—" The large pond

in Place Yard was doubtless originally designed for supplying the monastery with fish, as well as the moats in the
Horse-close. Near the entrance of the garden is a smaller
water, perhaps once a stew, where the fish were preserved for
immediate use, as the multiplicity of feasts in the Romish
calendar demanded a perpetual supply. The resources of the
priory were very large, and comprised lands at Kirtlington,
Missenden, Stratton, Audley, Bicester, and many other places."

It may be interesting to mention that the estates which lay
at Bicester and Wretchwick, on the beautiful road to Ambrosden,
were purchased by the family of Glynne, who resided here.
A son of the distinguished judge, who enjoyed the favour
both of Cromwell and Charles II., erected a noble mansion at
Ambrosden, and his son sat in Parliament for Woodstock.
In the early part of the eighteenth century the Glynnes
retired to their estate at Hawarden. The last of the male
line was the accomplished Sir Stephen Glynne, who died suddenly in London; and the large estates passed by marriage
to the family of the Right Hon. W. E. Gladstone.

Bicester Manor was at one time the property of Sir John
Le Strange and Jacquet his wife, daughter to Earl Rivers.
Joane, the daughter and heiress of the family, married George,
heir of the first Lord Derby, and so Bicester Manor passed
into the hands of the Stanleys. Some of the lands afterwards
belonged to Bicester Priory, and were sold to Serjeant Glynne,
who also purchased Hawarden Castle.

Stanley of Bicester figured prominently in the battle of
Bosworth. Richard thought that he was on his side; but as
he was married to the mother of the Earl of Richmond, who
was afterwards Henry VII., this very naturally led to
suspicion, and the old "History of Bicester" says that "he

refused Lord Stanley permission to retire into the country till he had given up Lord Strange as a pledge for his fidelity. But even this did not prevent his finally acting against that monarch.

The manor and estates of Bicester had passed in regular succession from Gilbert Basset (who founded the priory)

BICESTER CHURCHYARD.

through several females, but strictly according to the laws of primogeniture, to the first Earl of Derby.

Bicester Church is a very interesting building, and though restored it has not been spoiled—repaired would be a juster word to use regarding it. The grouping of the chancel end is pleasing, and shows a chancel higher than the nave. The length of this church is a hundred and twenty-five feet, and

the breadth, including the aisles, sixty-five.   To keep in
remembrance the prelates who were burned at Oxford, and
not long after their death, a huge volume of Foxe's "Martyrs"
was chained to a desk in the chancel of the church.   There
are a great number of monuments and quaint inscriptions inside
the building, and the churchyard contains many old tombstones.

BICESTER MARKET.

Bicester is an excellent specimen of an ancient market-
town, and the block of buildings here shown stands alone and
clear in the market-place ; nor are they of inconsiderable size.
Speaking from recollection, they must represent at least
twenty-five tenements.   There is a very similar block at
Richmond, in Yorkshire, and, indeed, they are not uncommon.
A large space has been left vacant, and in ages long gone by
those who had or who took the power utilised a part of it.

One of the buildings has the date of 1698 on a curious kind of
tower, but it stands among gables of much greater antiquity.
The promenade on the top is curious, and continually used by
the tenants in summer weather.   In the courtyard of the

ANCIENT DOVECOTE, BICESTER.

" King's Arms " is a splendid specimen of a wistaria.   This
hostelry would seem to be the head-quarters of the Bicester
Hunt, which has been established for nearly a century.   Any
one staying till the evening at Bicester will notice the large
flights of pigeons that come home to an ancient dovecote.
This is shown here, and is let with a farm near the church.

Dovecotes used to form a very valuable adjunct to a monastery, and might in certain localities be used with great advantage again. Only, however, in certain localities, for in a corn-growing district they are too destructive; but in some parts of England, where root-crops and hay form the more general articles of cultivation, they might be profitable, and in any parts where there are considerable beech-woods, they could provide for themselves with very little help. In America they congregate in vast numbers—numbers, indeed, beyond what we should think credible in this country—and they especially delight in those localities where there are clearings and culti-vated lands along the edges of a forest. They soon find out the patches of beech, and congregate in them; but at night and morning they fly away to seek new pastures; sometimes these are, to the dismay of the farmers, in cultivated land, and sometimes they pass over fields and homesteads to reach solitary beech-woods beyond.

They resemble wild ducks, in leaving their feeding-grounds early and late, and they fly in small, detached flocks, at a great speed—a speed far beyond what we should credit them with; for their stroke with their wings is not rapid, like that of a wild duck or a game-bird, but its grip of the air is exceedingly strong. A cutting from a London daily paper, which appeared when this was written, is curiously *à propos*:—"A race took place from Dover to London, between the Continental mail express train and a carrier-pigeon, conveying an urgent document for the French police. The rails, carriages, and engine of the express train were, as might be expected, of the best possible construction for power and speed." The pigeon, which was known as a "Belgian voyageur," had been homed when only a few weeks old, to a building in Cannon Street,

City. The bird was tossed through the railway-carriage window by a French official as the train left the Admiralty Pier, the wind being west, and the atmosphere hazy. The train had made more than a mile before the poor pigeon decided in its mind which direction to take, but it circled up in the air, rising all the time in wider rings, while the train, which made no stoppage, was speeding along at sixty miles an hour, and the railway officials laid any odds on their train with such of their friends as would take them up; indeed, some, of a sporting turn, wished to improve the opportunity, by laying a venture on the length of time it would be in before the pigeon was heard of. But the race was not to the strong, for a telegram announced the arrival of the bird twenty minutes before the train was heard of!

American wood-pigeons afford very pretty shooting, in the morning and evening, as they pass in little flights of some five or six; which flights increase in numbers as the day declines. Often they pass so quickly, that shots are lost every time a cartridge is being put into the gun.

These dovecotes are extremely interesting, and, according to that charming writer, Bishop Stanley, they produce enormous flocks of birds. He says that 15,000 have been the increase, in four years, from a single pair of birds. The conditions must have been extraordinarily favourable, both for their protection and their food; but the author speaks from his own very reliable knowledge. Perhaps, however, it might be well to say that his candour and truth may have accepted too readily certain narratives of flights of these birds which are found in some American authors. One he relates in his excellent book on birds; and, to quote his words—"The following calculation, made by a very accurate observer, places the subject, as far as relates to American wood-pigeons, in a still more striking point of view. He saw a column of pigeons, one mile in breadth, moving at the rate of one mile a minute, which, as it was four hours in passing, made the whole length 240 miles. He then calculated that each square yard of this moving body contained three pigeons, which thus gave 2,230,272,000 pigeons! And yet this he considered to be less than the real number. Computing each of these to consume half a pint of seed daily, the whole quantity would equal 17,424,000 bushels per day."

Now, this is quoted from a very delightful naturalist on birds. Audubon's works will always be justly admired and read; but even his ardent admirers—and they are many, quite including, for what the value of such testimony may be, the writer—do think this frequently-repeated tale wants a little confirmation. Perhaps, like the predictor of some eclipse or comet, he has left a cipher out in some of the lines, and the phenomenon has not appeared at the right time. But, at any rate, taking the figures as they stand, the result would show that this particular flock of pigeons, according to calculations that are not my own, consumed seed which, if weighed against wheat or any other cereal—which it might fairly be supposed to represent—would feed, certainly, Great Britain and Ireland, for three months. And Bishop Stanley adds, that a rapidity of flight has been, "wisely and graciously, given to these birds," to range over vast tracts of uncultivated earth, or else they would either have perished, or devoured up the productions of the farmers and the forests.

The subject would not have been dwelt on at such length, but the dovecotes are met with so frequently in Oxfordshire, that it is evident they formed at one time a valuable source of profit; we not unfrequently see them near old farmhouses, and very commonly indeed near monastic remains. It is probable that at one time the beeches and oaks of Wychwood, Wytham, Woodstock, and other forests provided them with the principal part of their sustenance, and they were taken from their roosts by thousands and sent to market. There are two very picturesque ones at Stanton Harcourt, one of which figures at the end of the chapter; and an excellent example of the ancient dovecote may be seen at Wytham. They were the objects of special care in monastic houses, often being of great size and elaborate construction.

The Royal Commission for the publication of the historic manuscripts in the possession of ancient families and corporations, include these items in their interesting series from Queen's College, 1326 :—"For making an earthen wall, $3\frac{1}{2}$ perches long, between the pigeon-house and the wall of the Friars' outhouses, by the piece, 2s. 9d.; for covering the same, and another wall on the other side of the pigeon-house, with straw, by the piece, 18d." The same papers convey an interesting account of the prices of building materials :—"To a plumber, for melting the lead of the old gutter, and melting the sheets for the new gutter, for one week, with victuals from the master, 18d.; for 24,000 lath-nails, for the roof, 16s. $3\frac{1}{2}$d." "Given to a certain poor man, as compensation for a wound accidentally received from a boar belonging to the house, 18d." These items refer to a grange at Southampton.

Dr. Plot, in his interesting history of the natural productions of Oxford, mentions a certain saline spring in the county, which is so attractive to the pigeons that abound in the various dovecotes, that he gravely says it would be a lucrative speculation to build a dovecote there, and so attract all the birds of the neighbourhood. Still, he admits that it would hardly be the "straight" thing to do, and says that, as he cannot quite recommend it on the *meum* and *tuum* principle, he will tell them another use the waters may be put to. Dr. Plot was Professor of Chemistry at Oxford, and, doubtless, the foremost chemist of the day; and we wonder if another century and three-quarters will see as great an advance in chemistry as there has been since he wrote.

The village of Eynsham may be readily reached along the Witney road from Oxford, but perhaps the more pleasant way is to take the railway to Yarnton Junction, and a short walk through Cassington will find it. Yarnton itself is very well worth a visit, and the church, with its altar tombs, is extremely interesting. Formerly it was attached to the Abbey of Eynsham; and there is the shaft of a stone cross of great interest in the churchyard, with figures of saints carved in it. Alderman Fletcher, who died in 1826, is said to be buried here in the coffin that once held Fair Rosamond's remains.

If we leave Yarnton and travel on the Eynsham road, we soon arrive at the quaint village of Cassington, which contains a church with a tall spire that can be seen from Oxford. There is a chancel to this church that dates back to the twelfth century, and several interesting brasses inside. This church was founded by the chamberlain of Henry II., who had much business in the neighbourhood. In this steeple, as at Kidlington, the junction between the tower and spire is rather abrupt, and it seems to stand in want of pinnacles and brooches to ease the lines of its tapering. This is by no means a difficult matter for any architect; he has only to look at some spire where this is deficient and another where it has been attended to, and he will at once see in how many ways it can be accomplished.

The engraving gives a very good idea of the cheerful, bright little village, with its quaint cross. This structure is of

CROSS AT EYNSHAM.

considerable antiquity—greater than we commonly find in any crosses that have escaped destruction. They rarely date further back than the fourteenth century—few, indeed, are of this antiquity—but Eynsham is apparently of the thirteenth century.

There are no remains of Eynsham Abbey; a few stones

may be seen that have probably belonged at one time to it.
So lately, however, as 1843, some considerable portions were
left.   This abbey was dissolved in 1539 ; and the last of the
abbots, who seems to have been as submissive as his brother of
Abingdon, was rewarded by being made the Bishop of Llandaff,
a city which was probably not quite so dismal in those days as
it is now.

That formidable stranger, the "American weed," as it is
called (*Anacharis alsinastrum*), obtained a strong footing here
—if, indeed, such a method of domiciling could be applied to
a plant that seemed to be independent of roots or ground-
hold at all; for though, unhappily, like couch-grass, it grows
from a small fragment, it grows on the surface of the water.
It had not been introduced into England for more than ten
years when it threatened almost to destroy the whole system
of internal navigation.   Frequently the traffic of slow rivers
was obstructed, the currents of minor streams impeded, and
isolated ponds were even filled up.   Some parts of the Thames,
especially near Eynsham, were only traversed with difficulty.

Mr. William Marshall, of Ely, in a small pamphlet, has
given its history so far as it is known.   It is so unlike any
other water-plant that it may be easily recognised.   Its leaves
are of a dark green, and grow in threes round a slender stringy
stem.   They are about half an inch long and egg-shaped, and
they are beset with minute teeth that enable them to cling to
anything.   The powers of propagation this plant possesses are
prodigious, for if a fragment only is broken off the stem it
will adhere to any object it comes in contact with, and spread
out in all directions indefinitely.   It becomes at once an
independent plant with roots and stems.   Indeed, it does not
wait even for a resting-place, but grows as it travels slowly

down the stream ; and if we add that the stems are remarkably brittle and easily broken, that completes a heavy list of indictments against it. Mr. Marshall considers it is of American importation, and has come over with a cargo of timber, the logs having collected specimens of it as they floated in rafts down the western river to Quebec. This may be the case, for plants resembling it in appearance have been found in American waters, but none that possess all its bad habits. He said, writing some years ago, that it would be impossible to eradicate it from our island, and all we could hope to do was to keep it under, if even that were possible ; for all known means by which weeds in water were subdued were useless in its case, or, to speak more truly, assisted to scatter it more widely. In some parts of England the meadows and rivers were all alike— one great expanse of green—and from an eminence it was hardly possible to tell where water-courses lay—

"Jamque mare et tellus nullum discrimen habebant"—

but when matters began to look almost hopeless, relief came from an unexpected quarter, and an early death terminated its dissipated career. It was probably almost *sui generis*, or had altered so much crossing the seas that in changing its sky it had changed its animus too, and found its grave in England.

Not far from here is the University paper mill. It will be remembered by every one how comparatively modern paper is apt to decay. The demand upon every kind of paper material has increased so rapidly that inferior stuff, and perhaps less costly methods of manufacture, have to be employed. This the Oxford University has met by establishing a manufactory of its own, where there is no fear of any article being turned out that is not well able to preserve valuable manuscripts. Let any one look on their own library shelves, and he will find abundant illustrations of this. What a boon it would be if more pains were taken generally over ink. There are missals in the library of the cathedral where this is written some four or five hundred years old, and the ink is as black and even brilliant as it was the day it was put on.

Some one, writing to *Notes and Queries*, mentions that in Oxford about twenty years ago a very black ink was sold in sixpenny and shilling stone bottles, which bottles were in the form of a monk, though these have disappeared. The ink in question was made by the enterprising firm of Messrs. Akermann, and is stated to be the result of a recipe found in a monastery. This note, however, brought one or two others on the subject of ink ; and mention is made of a charter in which Richard Cumyn, in 1170, conveyed certain lands, and after 700 years the ink is jet black and the finest strokes distinct.

The following is from the writings of the monk Rogerus, and must be nearly contemporaneous with the Norman Conquest.

" To make ink, cut for yourself wood of the thorn-trees in April or May, before they produce flowers or leaves, and collecting them in small bundles, allow them to lie in the shade for two, three, or four weeks, until they are somewhat dry. Then have wooden mallets, with which you beat these thorns upon another piece of hard wood until you peel off the bark everywhere, put which immediately into a barrelful of water. When you have filled two, or three, or four, or five barrels with bark and water, allow them to stand for eight days, until the water imbibes all the sap of the bark. Afterwards put the water into a very clean pan or into a cauldron, and fire being placed under it, boil it ; from time to time, also, throw into the pan some of this bark, so that whatever sap may remain in it may be boiled out.   When you have cooked it a little, throw it out and again put in more ; which done, boil down the remaining water into a third part, and then, pouring it out of this pan, put it into one smaller, and cook it until it grows black and begins to thicken ; add one-third part of pure wine, and putting it into two or three new pots, cook it until you see a sort of skin show itself on the surface ; then taking these pots from the fire, place them in the sun, until the black ink purifies itself from the red dregs.   Afterwards take small bags of parchment, carefully sewn, and bladders, and pouring in the pure ink, suspend them in the sun until all is quite dry, and when dry, take from it as much as you wish, and temper it with wine over the fire ; and, adding a little vitriol, write.   But if it should happen, through negligence, that your ink be not black enough, take a fragment of the thickness of a finger, and putting it into the fire, allow it to glow, and throw it directly into the ink."

DOVECOTE, STANTON HARCOURT.

CHAPTER VII.

Queen Kath.　　　　　　Come, reverend fathers,
Bestow your counsels on me ; now she begs
That little thought when she set footing here,
She should have bought her dignities so dear.—*Henry VIII.*

From Eynsham to Cumnor—Amy Robsart and her History—Sir Walter Scott and his Description of Cumnor—Aged Butler to Pembroke College, and his Recollections of Old Cumnor—Stained Glass at Wytham—Stained Glass and Old Designers—Witney— Witney Blankets—Witney Cross.

From Eynsham, a pleasant walk to the west of Wytham Hill, past Moor's Farm, Filchamstead, and Smith's Brake, brings us into the village of Cumnor, in Berks ; it is beautifully situated, and a pleasant object to see on every side from which it can be approached. It is well shaded over, and always very clean. Of course, it owes much of its celebrity to the pages of Sir Walter Scott.

The history of poor Amy Robsart has often been told, and it is more than probable that the commonly received version is the correct one, or, at any rate, quite as nearly so as the distance of time would lead one to expect.

Amy Robsart was the daughter of Sir John Robsart, of Sheen Court, in Surrey ; and I took the opportunity of writing a line to the excellent publication, *Notes and Queries*, to ascertain if any one could give further information concerning her family, and it seems that Sir John Robsart was the son of Sir Terry Robsart, who was at Calais with Edward IV., and his name often occurs in the Pasten Letters, which were written

about the beginning of the sixteenth century. These letters
have been happily instanced as a proof of the intellectual
vigour that underlays the surface of the useless learning which
characterised the scholars of the day. The numberless works
on alchemy and the philosopher's stone, on magic, or the elixir
of life, that abounded in that time, show like a fungus growth
the decay of mental vigour in its proper branches. The Pasten
Letters, which are simply the preserved correspondence of the
Pasten family, display a fluency and vivacity, as well as a gram-
matical correctness, which would have been very unusual in
familiar letters a hundred years before. Sir Terry Robsart's
name continually occurs in these letters; he was settled at Shir-
land, in Kent, and his name often occurs in connection with
Sir John Scott, Comptroller of the Household of Edward IV.,
and Marshal of Calais.

His son, Sir John Robsart, married Elizabeth Scott, of
Appleyard, county Norfolk, and daughter of Edward Scott, of
the mansion of Mote, Sussex. A direct descendant of the Scott
family is living, and he obligingly furnished me with the particulars. Amy Robsart was the daughter of Sir John Robsart
and Elizabeth Scott.

Robert Dudley was only the third son of the Duke of
Northumberland, who had been guilty of so much wrong, and
was beheaded in the reign of Queen Mary; and he himself was
a not unworthy son of his sire, guilty of more crimes and
murders, in all probability, than it would be pleasant now to
trace or rake up in memory.

Elizabeth's partiality for a comely form is a matter of
history; and with his usual felicity Thackeray has sketched
her visit to Crawley, where she met the Crawley of the period,
who presented her on his knee with a tankard of fine

Hampshire ale on a hot summer's day, and as he possessed a well-formed calf, which his position set off effectively, Her Majesty at once made him a baronet, and the place was called Queen's Crawley ever after.

Elizabeth's delight in all matters of display and splendour are memorable; she moved from castle to castle, as has been recently said, as through a series of gorgeous pageants, "fanciful and extravagant as a caliph's dream. A happy retort or a finished compliment never failed to win her favour. She would dance a coranto, that the French ambassador, hidden dexterously behind a curtain, might report her sprightliness to his master." The same accurate authority states that personal beauty in a man was a sure passport to her favour, that she patted young squires—if they were handsome—on the neck when they knelt to kiss her hand, and fondled her "sweet Robin" on the neck in the face of the Court—which soubriquet she used to employ towards her favourite, the handsome Earl of Leicester. Indeed, it is probable that whatever tenderness it was in the power of her nature to possess was centred in her worthless favourite. Still, we may always feel a degree of gratitude to him for having founded the hospital that bears his name in Warwick, and is, with its gate and chapel, the most delightful picture of the entrance to an old English town that we possess. There is so very much of it. Canterbury Gate is beautiful, but it is the entrance to the precincts of the cathedral in reality, and only stretches across the street; but the Leicester Gate is a combination of chapel, hospital, and archway all in one.

That such a man as Leicester could have easily gained the daughter of a country squire is readily understood; and there can be little doubt that Amy Robsart's beauty was great, and, as Mickle's plaintive ballad says, that in her father's hall it "well was prized."

Sir Walter Scott's account of her secret marriage unknown to her father, and her being spirited away from Sheen Court, are poetical licenses, for she was well endowed both by her father and her father-in-law, as is shown by the very valuable results of the Royal Commission that has been appointed to collect the historic documents which have been preserved in private families.

There is an interesting document at Longleat, in Wiltshire, the venerable seat of the Marquis of Bath, that alludes to a marriage settlement between the parents; and in the same library is a letter from Amy Robsart to her "tailor," respecting an account, which seems, singularly enough, only to have been discharged after her death.

There is in the library, under date 1550, an original deed of settlement, between John Dudley, Earl of Warwick, and Sir John Robsart, Kt., "in contemplation of the marriage between Robert Dudley, one of the younger sons (afterwards the Earl of Leicester), and Amye, daughter of Sir John Robsart." The earl settles Cokkesford Priory lands, couuty Norfolk, on Robert and Amye and the heirs of the body of Robert, and also an annuity of £50 during the singleness of Lady Mary (afterwards Queen Mary). Sir John Robsart covenants to settle some lands on Amye and Robert and the heirs of the body of Amye, also an annuity of £20 during the singleness of Lady Mary; and one would fancy that the position of the Robsarts must have been considerable, before any one who had an eye on the throne for his family, and made provision accordingly, could have consented to such an arrangement.

After reading this document of such undoubted authenticity,

I referred to the history of Cokkesford in "Dugdale," and was rather surprised to find that the Cokkesford lands were given by Henry VIII. to the Duke of Northumberland. He obtained a charter, in the reign of Elizabeth, to convey them to the Townshend family, in whose possession they still remain. Probably, further knowledge would enable one to reconcile the discrepancy; but there it is. There is also an interesting letter in the same collection from the Earl of Leicester to Anthony Foster, giving him directions for the dining-room at Killingworth.

Sir Walter Scott speaks of Cumnor as "pleasantly built on a hill; and in a wooded park closely adjacent was situated the ancient mansion, of which the ruins may be still extant. The park was full of large trees, and in particular of ancient and mighty oaks, which stretched their giant arms over the high wall surrounding the demesne, thus giving it a melancholy, secluded, and monastic appearance. The entrance to the park lay through an old-fashioned gateway in the outer wall, the door of which was formed of two oaken leaves, thickly studded with nails, like the gate of an old tower. A large orchard surrounded the house on two sides, though the trees, abandoned by the care of man, were overgrown and mossy, and seemed to bear little fruit. Those that had been formerly trained as espaliers had resumed their natural mode of growing, and exhibited grotesque forms, partaking of the original training which they had received." It may be worth remark, however, that espaliers retain their form for great periods of time. I saw rows of them once in a garden in Shropshire that belonged formerly to an abbey, and though the stems of the fruit-trees were thick and gnarled, the straight lines were preserved exactly all along the rows, and must have had

WYTHAM CHURCH.

generations of careful culture before they could have retained
such exquisite exactness after several centuries of partial neglect.
There are now few remains of Cumnor Hall at Cumnor, but
some stained glass has been removed to Wytham Abbey and
Wytham Church; and the gateway shown on the right hand
of the engraving is a relic of Cumnor Hall. It was probably

CUMNOR CHURCHYARD.

not the entrance gateway, but some postern in the grounds leading either to a garden or farm-buildings. Cumnor Church is
delightfully situated in a wooded country, and the transept
here shown can have undergone little change since it was built,
and it was two centuries old when it was a familiar object to
Amy Robsart.

This church contains a Latin inscription to Anthony Foster,
and a monument. The inscription enumerates his many

virtues : his eloquence, piety, activity, patriotism, and benevolence, and other estimable qualities for which posterity does not seem to have given him due credit.

There is also the usual chained Bible. These are much more common in country churches than is sometimes supposed, though I never met with any satisfactory account of the origin of their being so bound. If it was simply to preserve them from pilfering hands of friends who wished to study the contents at home, the fact of their zeal might have been considered as a safeguard against their breaking the Eighth Commandment ; but if it was to protect them against marauders, the fastenings were entirely inadequate. It is to be hoped, however, that such of these relics as are left will not share the fate of a " restored " one I heard of. The old chain was struck off; the book rebound elegantly in imitation vellum ; and the whole taken from an ancient pew to a light-brown new oak reading-desk, with a sham silver chain in place of the worn wrought-iron one. There it was shown as " our celebrated chained Bible."

The body of Amy Robsart was buried nearly at the east door of St. Mary's Church, in Oxford, and Dr. Babington (Lord Leicester's chaplain) preached her funeral sermon ; and if confirmation of the way in which she is generally supposed to have met her death were required, it would be in the fact that, at the request of her father, the coroner ordered the body to be exhumed, and an examination made : though, under all circumstances, it was hardly likely that any verdict against Leicester and his party would be given ; but the verdict, such as it was, is a tolerably clear proof of the unhappy tale that has obtained credence, for " accidentally slain " was quite as much as could have been expected, however clear the proofs had been. The verdicts of the time were generally well worded — many, at least, with which I have met—for they were given by direction of the coroner, and the fact that the word "slain" was admitted in such a sentence speaks volumes.

It was my fortune to meet with an old resident of Cumnor, who formerly held the situation of butler to Pembroke College, and his recollections of that college were interesting, though, as he had numbered ninety-eight summers, and was just on the point of scoring one more when I met with him in a pleasant, old-fashioned farmhouse, one felt naturally rather inclined to let him speak of subjects that were not so carefully chronicled as college records. He well remembered Cumnor Hall, or "Cumnor Place," as it was more commonly called, and it abutted upon the high road leading to Abingdon. Some traces of the walls are left towards the road, and the school-house is built behind what fragments there are; but they have no interest. Within the last half century, however, chimneys were standing that seemed almost to defy the spoiler—or at least, so my informant said—and they were only knocked down with great labour at last. The trees in the park, which stretched away to the back of the manor, were elms, and not oaks as Scott and Mickle have stated. He well remembered the chapel in which grain was stored, and it led out to Cumnor churchyard. This is not an uncommon feature in old houses. A parish church will abut upon some manor-house; and though the former may contain a private chapel belonging to the family who reside there, they have not unfrequently a chapel in the house itself as well. This aged chronicler mentioned a curious circumstance that illustrates the last verse in "Cumnor Hall":—

> "And in that manor now no more
> Is merry feast or sprightly ball;
> For ever since that dreary hour
> Have spirits haunted Cumnor Hall."

There were some fish-ponds, now filled up, and he used often to fish there with his schoolmates; but when the day drew towards evening he remembers how a general flight could

WYTHAM INN.

be extemporised by any one calling, "Madam Dudley is coming!"

The old "Black Bear" is different from the house that now is called by that name, and stood nearly opposite the church.

It was a much more homely place than the sumptuous hostelry that Scott has described, and contained only six apartments in all. At any rate, it is much to be regretted that a building which has figured so conspicuously in romance and history was not allowed to remain, when a few loads of sand and lime would have preserved it in its entirety to the present day.

The stained glass at Wytham Church is only slight, and consists of some armorial bearings that appear to have belonged to the Dudley family, and a Scripture scene; indeed, the stained glass remains round Oxford seem to have suffered more than might have been looked for in such a locality. In Gloucestershire they are numerous; and there are some few good examples in Berkshire; but one would have expected to find more in Oxford. The old ones that remain are very good, and quite fulfil the necessary requirements that seem to have so constantly guided ancient designers to excellence. The old idea of stained glass was that a window was intended to let in the light, and anything that interfered with this condition was against its usefulness. In the best examples—as we see, for example, in York—the light is not hindered; and Gray's description of a "rich window that obscures the light" no more applies to a good stained window than his allusion to a passage which leads to nothing corresponds with a lobby in an ordinary dwelling. Perhaps it may not be quite out of place to allude to some of the old principles. It was well understood that a window was to be looked through, and not at, as a picture is; and here the power of stained glass is most clearly indicated. For example, let us take a picture—say, the most brilliant landscape that any artist ever painted—and on a bright day place this in the best light that can be found for it. Now, if we look at this picture till we can quite feel its glow and lightness, and

then suddenly look through the window, we shall at once see
that the picture labours under sad odds : the ray of light we
catch is almost blinding ; and if we look at the picture after contemplating the window, it is only a dull, leaden, heavy mass of
grey. This at once shows how different the conditions are
between a stained glass window and a shaded picture. The
object of the stained glass designer ought to be, in the first
place, to procure the brightest and most transparent of tints.
A very accomplished gentleman, belonging to the Inner Temple,
spent much time in endeavouring to find out the secrets of the
rich hues of the twelfth, thirteenth, and sixteenth centuries, or
rather, found his greatest success to lie in the discoveries he
made of these periods. He at once disposed of the idea that
the mellow rich tones were the result of age, because he
submitted some pieces of ancient glass to alkali, and found that
after the glass was so cleaned it was still superior in depth of
colour to any modern specimens. This gentleman possessed
abundant leisure and opportunity for having his experiments
conducted by eminent chemists, and succeeded in reproducing
some of the purest and best colours of antiquity. He quite
revived the ancient blue, the streaky ruby, the whites and
yellows, and several, but not all, the greens. But he sadly
admitted that his labours would probably be of little use, for
the manufacturers who conducted his experiments succeeded in
producing through his labours a cheaper article for their own
purposes. There has long been a traditional belief that the
gorgeous blue in the clerestory of York was made with *lapis-
lazuli*, but it was found by simple experiments on glass of similar
hue to have been produced from cobalt. And those who are
acquainted with the glorious tints of that clerestory can well
understand the traditions which long lingered in the alleys

round Stonegate and Sampson Square—and indeed are not discredited yet—that supposed precious stones are set in the lead
bindings. Thin slices of ruby and emerald are doubtless found
in Continental churches, and are properly set off to attract the
eye from any point of vision. But probably the secret of the
beauty of our English stained glass lies much in the knowledge
of distribution of tints with neutral grounds. The meaning of
such an obscure solution is probably illustrated thus :—Close
the shutters and darken a room, and then through some small
aperture allow a thin ray of light to penetrate. The rays of
this light will be dissolved into all the colours, and these will
be a certain index to the various tints that should be employed
where stained glass is to be used, in the order in which one
piece of coloured glass succeeds another. But how could such
a principle be employed in practice ? any one may, with reason,
ask ; for though it is certain that the refraction of light in a
many-coloured window alters the tints and sometimes deadens
them, could any known or even unknown system bring a stained
glass window always into harmony with the theory indicated ?
Well, certainly not ; and though a hundred schools might be
founded, and all of them never exceeded the limits of truth, the
very conditions of cross lights and surroundings would effectually
kill every kind of system and reduce it to empiricism. And
often I have thought, in drawing on the blocks that illustrate
this work, what untold histories are written in their sections!
A block of wood for engraving is the cross-cut of an Asiatic
boxwood tree, and the rings that appear in most of those which
have been employed in the present instance refer us back in
their tiny circumferences to the time when Philip of Spain
proposed to introduce the Spanish Inquisition into our
uncongenial soil. Many theories might be adduced by their

rings of varied breadth; and years of heat or cold or moisture, perhaps of pestilence and famine, in Circassia are certainly, in some measure, indicated. But any historical theory on such slender evidence—however free from the charge of prejudice it would be—could hardly be valuable. So if we endeavour to reduce the theory of a stained glass window into any limits beyond the very broadest, we are sure to land in confusion.

There is no doubt at all that every principle of colour and its combinations is at work; but the successful man must feel his way for himself, and though he cannot study or learn too much, he must be able to say with Ovid in his banishment,

" Et quod tentabam scribere, versus erat."

Generally speaking, however, the brilliant whites should predominate, and the actual stained glass, which in the best examples of antiquity never exceeds a fourth or, at the outside, a third of the surface, should be as brilliant as possible. The subdued tints are more suitable for some country where the sky is brighter; and if figures are introduced, one single expression, intensified as much as possible, should prevail. In the earlier examples, corresponding with what we should call Early English in architecture, and indeed for some time after, the most beautiful and the deepest tints only were used; one plane only is represented, and there is hardly any attempt at a background. In the few instances where this was introduced, it is in the same positive colours as the foreground, and so apparently in the same plane. All the objects are in a strong black outline, and the shadow was in a half tint. This mode of treatment gave intense brilliancy, almost resembling a transparent mosaic. In the fifteenth century an advance is made towards perspective and light and shade, and in later

times a further attempt is made to approximate a window to
an oil-painting; but the early glass is the most effective, and
most truly fills its required place in architecture.   But however
pleasant wayside reveries may be, we are in the way to Witney
and Minster Lovell, and a walk through a not very interesting
country of some five miles will land us in Witney.

Witney is a remarkably pleasant old town, and though
still very cheerful, especially on market-days, it bears all the
traces of bygone prosperity.   Four thousand persons were once,
it is said, employed on the looms, while now, I was told, there
are not 200 hands.   There is always something melancholy
in departed prosperity; perhaps one of the most striking
features of Louvain, for example, is the disparity of the city to
its inhabitants : even though so much has there fallen into
ruin, still, a population can hardly lapse from 150,000 to 30,000
without leaving traces of its decay.   Witney is not quite in
so melancholy a plight as this, though we may be here and
there surprised at finding a Tudor doorway with cusped
panels.   Witney blankets are celebrated all over the world;
they are well known in New York and San Francisco, and in
Melbourne and Jamaica.   Indeed, the few drying-poles where
the blankets are still prepared astonish a travelled stranger who
expects to see some mighty industry.   But this is common to
all manufactures of celebrity.   Everton is a suburb of Liverpool, and in a small thatched cottage there the world-renowned
toffee is made.   Ormskirk, also, which was till lately a sleepy
little market-town in Lancashire, has connected its name with
the most approved gingerbreads, though cynics and even
experts say that vast quantities of these confections of equal
quality are sold in London every year that never saw either
Everton or Ormskirk.   Probably, however, Witney blankets

do not profess to come from Witney, any more than Brussels carpets from Brussels. It may be only a legal fiction among manufacturers. At the end of the long street is the parish church of the Trinity. It is a splendid cruciform structure— indeed, one of the finest in the whole county. The living is of great value, and in the gift of the Bishop of Winchester. The view of Witney Church here is from the side that faces the enormous village green, and is an admirable example of effective church architecture. It too often happens now, with all our improved knowledge of Gothic, that one church follows another in design. Given, as it were, an order for a church to cost, let us say, £5,000 and to seat 300 people, any one who has kept his eye at all upon recent design could almost be sure to anticipate the result—a nave sixty feet long and thirty wide, and a chancel twenty-five feet long and eighteen wide, all in the clear; the nave spanned by five principals, and lit by an Early Decorated window between each pair; the window two-light, trefoiled, and having a trefoiled circular head; and the tower covered with a penthouse roof till money was raised for a spire. Till recently, anything different from this was considered rather below the mark; now, however, some of the more thoughtful architects have seen the many excellences of Perpendicular. Early English, to be effective in a modern building, is too costly. Perhaps the details of the view of Witney here given are not of the very highest character. The Norman doorway is plain; the Decorated window rather coarse in design; and the Early English tower and spire, though finely proportioned, do not afford very excellent specimens of the details of the style; but all this vanishes in the presence of the fine effect of the group. It looks so natural and massive, and so very free from studied effect.

WITNEY CHURCH.

The market cross at Witney is extremely curious, and, according to an inscription on the face, it was built in 1683, but it has the appearance of an older design: at least, if the restored state is an approximate copy of its original form. It

OLD BLANKET MARKET, WITNEY.

is a type of the covered market cross that at one time was so prevalent in England, and of which such splendid specimens are yet to be seen in Salisbury, Malmesbury, and Chichester. This is not the old blanket mart; the latter is now a brewery. The arms of the company appear on the clock in front of the ball, and are three leopards' heads and three roses. The crest is a leopard's head crowned with a ducal coronet, and the motto is, " Weave truth with trust."

Witney is celebrated, according to an old saying, for four B's —beauty, blankets, bread, and beer. The last three are doubtless excellent, and as for the first, every eye may be said to form its own standard. I chanced to be there on a market-day, when visitors from different parts were present and the streets were tolerably well filled. The knowledge that so many strangers were present would certainly be sufficient to prevent any dogmatic opinion on the subject, for Witney might be debited or credited unjustly.

Dr. Plot, the old historian of Oxford, attributes the whiteness of Witney blankets to the " nitrous Windrush," which joins the Isis at Newbridge. In 1711 the blanket-makers in the town and within twenty miles round were incorporated by the style of " Master, Assistants, Wardens, and Commonalty of the Blanket-weavers of Witney, in Oxfordshire," and about ten years afterwards the market alluded to before was built. Here the blankets were weighed, measured, and marked in accordance with the terms of the charter.

At Witney are the remains of Emma's Dyke or foss, though it is said that its object, or the cause of Queen Emma's name being connected with it, are involved in obscurity. Queen Emma married Ethelred the Unready, and one of her sons, Edward the Confessor, was born at Islip, in Oxford. She seems not to have lived very happily with her husband, and often apart from him. In a field near the church there is a house, called the Mount House, which seems to have been once fortified, and of which very little is known. All we can be certain of is that it was built at the

time when every man's house was literally his castle. Some
writers think that it was once a residence of the Bishops of
Winchester, and perhaps such a supposition is not entirely
without foundation. It is very probable that a list of the
various bishops' and abbots' palaces in England would astonish
any one who approached the subject for the first time. The
remains that even now exist, and are used either as farmhouses, or residences, or that are left—like the superb remains
at Lincoln or Southwell—in ruins, would afford abundant
material for a work that should supply every necessity of an
architectural library, and illustrate excellently all the styles
of English architecture.

It is said, I believe without exaggeration, that at the time
of the dissolution of the monasteries the clerical party were in
possession of half the wealth of England; and if any one will
carefully peruse any county guide in the country he will be
surprised at the number of dwelling-houses once pertaining to
the mitred abbots, and now so far diverted from their original
uses—whatever those uses may have been, and of which, indeed,
there is more than one theory. Shakespeare wrote one of his
most dramatic plays within only a comparatively short time of
the dissolution of monasteries, or, at any rate, when such an
event had not ceased to be a matter of common discourse; and
often we can find in his simplest phrases many a clue to the
sentiments of the day. Often the worldly wealth and magnificence of Churchmen must have formed the subject of conversa-
tions that Shakespeare heard among men who remembered
their profusion and contrasted their vast possessions with their
mission. So he perhaps only put such gossip into his own
language in the words Henry VIII. uses of Wolsey, when
speaking to Norfolk and Lovell. He had accidentally come

into possession of an inventory of the cardinal's vast
riches :—

> " What piles of wealth hath he accumulated
> To his own portion ! and what expense by the hour
> Seems to flow from him !   How i' the name of thrift
> Does he rake this together ? "

At any rate, Witney Manor has long been connected with the
Bishops of Winchester, and was given, with eight others, by
Aylwyn, Bishop of Winchester, to the cathedral church of that
city, out of gratitude, it is said, for being freed from some
charges that lay heavily upon him.

CHAPTER VIII.

" His eyes
Were with his heart, and that was far away.
He recked not of the life he lost, nor prize,
But where his rude hut by the Danube lay,
There were his young barbarians all at play,
There was their Dacian mother—he, their sire,
Butchered to make a Roman holiday."—*Byron.*

GABLE IN CORNMARKET STREET, OXFORD.

GROSE says that Minster Lovell Priory is not mentioned in "Dugdale." It appears, however, in the edition in Chester Cathedral library; and Leland, in his "Itinerary," describes it more as a mansion than a religious house. "Then about a myle to Mynster village having the name of Lovell, sometyme lord of it, there is an ancient place of the Lovells hardeby the churche. Master Vinlin, of Wadely, by Faringdon, hath it of the king in ferme." But unhappily, even since the sketch which appears in Grose, bearing date 1775, the few remains have suffered from the hands of the spoiler.

Dugdale describes it as an alien priory of Benedictine monks, and a cell to the monastery of Yvry, before *S. Johannis*; and after the suppression of alien houses it was granted to Eton College, which still retains it, the living being in the gift of the college, and worth, according to the Clergy List, some £200 per annum, with a residence. These estimates in the list are generally formed on the net income after the deductions for house and other necessary expenses.

Minster Lovell takes us back to the days of the Barons and the Wars of the Roses—the wars which for a century desolated England, and were so extremely senseless and objectless in their aim that a simple narrative of them would seem incredible. Between the merits of the two houses of York and Lancaster we, even at this distance, could not possibly desire to form any estimate. They may have had individual merits and fitness to rule among their leaders, but the circumstances by which they were surrounded developed very different qualities from these. Yet men were taken from their ploughs and crafts, without a murmur, to fight for a cause of which they knew nothing, and for which they cared less, and that in behalf of persons who would barely have admitted their title to be men of the same flesh and blood as themselves. They were slaughtered in thousands on each battle-field; and the halt and maimed are not catalogued. This, too, at a time when there were no great institutions like Greenwich or Chelsea, and certainly no union workhouses. The hospitals of the period were only like toys, so far as their real utility went, to meet the difficulties, and adorned the beneficence or bequests of some man of wealth. How those who escaped the carnage eked out a living may be gathered from an expression of Sir John Falstaff's; and, even making ever so much allowance for the estimate which his men of buckram will entitle us to do, the expression, "There's but

three of my hundred and fifty left alive, and they are for the
town's end to beg during life." How such a picture as this
peoples the entrance-gates of Warwick, or Coventry, or Chester!
Shakespeare wrote not very long after Bosworth Field, and, at
any rate, the traditions of sufferings must have been very fresh
in his time.

The facility with which allegiance was changed is told with
exceeding pathos in the last part of " Henry VI." Henry was
a man of whom Shakespeare, whether he would or no, has left
us some pleasant and plaintive recollections.

> "My crown is in my heart, not on my head ;
>   Not decked with diamonds and Indian stones,"

he says to the gamekeeper, on a north country moor, who had
captured him, and who asks him, if he be a king, where is his
crown? The keeper protests that he has sworn allegiance to
the king, and admits he has sworn the same to the deposed
monarch, but cannot see the point of Henry's question—"Where
did you dwell when I was King of England?" and argues they
were subjects *but* while he was king; to which Henry replies—

> " Look as I blow this feather from my face,
>   And as the air blows it to me again—
>   *   *   *   *   *
> Such is the lightness of you common men."

It almost passes belief that education was so low, or rather,
perhaps, that the power of the Barons was so supreme. The
Magna Charta was wrested, it is true, from King John by them :
but that was on their own account, not on the people's ; and, for
some time after, the fair lands of England were defaced by the
private vices of great nobles. The farmers and craftsmen
hardly desired to have any hand at all in the government of the

kingdom, and thought such things were only for nobles—"their betters" they called them; and it is a fact that the apathy lingers yet in many—indeed, perhaps most—rural districts. "I vote blue, Sir John," a farmer will say to his landlord at election times; "my father voted blue for your grandfather fifty years ago, and blue it shall always be with me;" while his next farm neighbour may be "red" for reasons of similar cogency and intelligence; but what "red" or "blue" is they never knew. They might say, as the French do of cricket, that it is a game they not only do not understand, but they would not like to.

This apathy is merely a reflection of the condition of the national mind during the Wars of the Roses, only that then it was deeper. The "passive obedience" had been instilled into them from earliest childhood, and fathers and sons on different estates were pressed for different sides, as at Towton, where a father kills his son, being the Earl of Warwick's man, and in another instance a son kills his father at the same battle; while each, in the fifth scene of the second act of "Henry VI.," expects to find plunder in the adversary that has so terribly fallen before their sword.

Now, if Shakespeare could bring before us Cæsar or Antony in their characters, and make them pass over the stage "alive and real," as no scholar has ever done, is it not more than probable that his details of the Wars of the Roses are correct? Bosworth Field, the last of them, was fought only eighty years before he was born, and his great-grandfather received a grant of lands after it.

Falstaff, who is always a favourite of Shakespeare's, just as much as Costigan is of Thackeray's, seems to have gone through the country, and collected men, or, rather, supplies, anywhere.

MINSTER LOVELL: RUINS OF THE HALL.

He says on one occasion he has got for a hundred and fifty soldiers three hundred and odd pounds. " I press me none," he says, " but good householders, yeomens' sons, such as had been asked twice on the banns; such a commodity of warm slaves as had as lief hear the devil as a drum; such as fear the report of a caliver worse than a struck fowl or a hurt wild duck. I pressed me none but toasts and butter, with hearts in their bellies no bigger than pins' heads, and they have bought out their services." This graphic description of the way in which the press-gang could be used to bring up neighbours to fight neighbours, and relatives relatives, is of more value than volumes of statistics, even saying nothing about the misuse of the power. Perhaps some would think this is the least objectionable feature, as it did afford some way of getting out of conscription.

The manor-house at Minster Lovell was the residence of the Lord Lovel who was a too willing servant of Richard III., and it figures in Clara Reeves' novel, " Old English Barons." There was not much in him to admire; and the mansion has a rather gloomy look, in spite of its beautiful situation in the charming valley of the Windrush. The details of the windows are very beautiful, and the mouldings of the doors and the groining leave nothing to take any exception to. Then the very gloominess is not more than is common to noblemen's houses of the period, when they were timidly emerging from fortified castles. The place is not easy to trace out, but it must have been very extensive; and the village itself bears remarkable traces of ancient wealth and prosperity: nearly every barn and dwelling-house is built of beautifully-dressed and squared stones, and though some may have been taken away from the ruins of the mansion-house, I should think these

were not many.   The masonry is too true and the stones too
well fitted into their places for such a thing, because it will
always be found that where stones are removed from an old
building to put into a more modern one, joints do not fit, and
there are gaps filled with mortar and inserted ashlar.   Here,
however, the character is quite different, and the ancient
masonry of the village is very beautiful.   There is a curious
sort of viaduct with small arches for the water to get away in
floods and leave the footpath dry.   Lord Lovel, Catesby, and
Ratcliff appear in "Richard III.," and do his bidding.   The old
couplet, written by Collingbourne—

> "The cat, the rat, and Lovell the dogge,
> Ruled all England under a hogge"—

cost the author his life.   This Lovel it was who appeared to
such disadvantage in the play, and was present when the
mocking Glo'ster said to the Bishop of Ely :—

> "My lord of Ely, when I was last in Holborn
> I saw good strawberries in your garden there;
> I do beseech you send for some of them."

Holinshed, speaking of the same scene, says that while the
council was sitting in the Tower, "First about nine of the
clock, saluting them courteously, and excusing himself that he
had been from them so long, saying merrily that he had been a
sleeper that day.   After a little talking with them, he said unto
the Bishop of Ely, 'My lord, you have very good strawberries
in your garden at Holborn; I require you let us have a mess of
them.'   'Gladly, my lord,' quoth he; 'would God I had
some better thing as ready to your pleasure as that.'"   And
then, of course, the bishop despatched a servant for them, who,
when he returned, found Hastings beheaded and his master in

the Tower under arrest. Glo'ster seems to have sworn that he would not dine until he had seen Hastings' head. Catesby says :—

> " Despatch—my Lord the King would be at dinner :
> Make a short shrift—he longs to see your head."

And Lovel, after wishing him good speed, hurried off into the Tower yard, returning to his master with Hastings' head, and alluding to the incorruptible minister as—

> " That ignoble traitor—
> The dangerous and unsuspected Hastings."

There seems to be little doubt about the authenticity of the tale concerning the strawberries, but some inaccuracy must have crept into the dates of the occurrence. The school histories of England speak of May 10th as the date of Hastings' execution. Perhaps this should read June, for the 22nd of June was the date fixed for the coronation of Edward by his treacherous uncle.

It is probable that Lovel was early in the secret of the pretender Lambert Simnel, who was born near his estate, and who proved fatal to him at last. He went to Ireland, where the Yorkists had many friends, and personated the Earl of Warwick, pretending that he made his escape from the Tower. Lovel took his part, and fought with him at the battle of Stoke-upon-Trent. He is said to have been drowned in crossing the Trent after the rout of Simnel, though the more popular and commonly believed tale is that he made his escape to Minster Lovell again, and secreted himself in a hidden room, where a trusty servant supplied him with the necessaries of life ; but the servant died suddenly and he perished for want. The only other partner to the secret was his faithful dog, which perished with him.

Gough believed this story, and says, in confirmation, that on one occasion the workmen employed at the hall opened up some secret chamber and found the body of a man in rich clothing seated in a chair, with a mass book before him on a table, and the remains of a dog by his side; but they crumbled when touched.   One is always reluctant to discredit any popular tale on the score of improbability, because many of the facts of history read so like overdrawn romances.   If any one were to have sat down when Fielding wrote "Tom Jones," and framed a romance that the son of a Corsican lawyer then living would make himself a great European emperor and all his brothers kings, the people would have said that he was rather out of date; and his works would have had a better chance of success, if not the possibility of running through several editions, provided they had been contemporaneous with the really entertaining adventures of Sinbad the Sailor.

But the objections to Gough's story—or such, at least as appears to lie on the face of it—are these: that a man dying of starvation would probably be lying down on the floor from exhaustion;   and furthermore, that he would not permit himself to be a prisoner without the means of exit, which he would surely have ventured upon using, especially, it may be added, as he must have heard that Simon the priest, who arranged the plots of Simnel, was not executed; and Simnel himself, with more humanity than might have been expected at the period, was made a scullion to the king.   Sagacity, perhaps, should be the word, instead of humanity; and it well consists with the monarch who had Warwick taken out of his captivity and paraded round London to allow any one who chose to speak to him to assure himself that Simnel was an impostor.   The same would soon be found from Simnel himself, in his more congenial work as a scullion, for it is generally believed that his father was a baker in Oxford.

These tales of imprisoning and dying of starvation are rather popular, and one that is connected with this locality may be considered a fair example. There was a sort of half-crazy man in Cheshire, called Nixon, and he used to prophesy various things connected with Cheshire families and the common-weal of England. He, as may be readily believed, made several rather successful guesses, and was sent for by King Henry IV. to be a kind of court prophet. The moment this witless person heard that he was required at the palace, he declared that he knew he would be "clemmed" there; and the general belief is that he was ordered especial care and consideration, but in some way the servants forgot him. The king had ordered a special room for him, and having offended the royal servants by his north-country ways, he was billeted off into this room, where he was forgotten when the king left Windsor for Woodstock. He here fulfilled the prophecy that the king had taken pains to avoid, and was found some time after starved to death. The tale is entirely believed to this day in Cheshire; and it is said the king entrusted the key of the room to a private body-servant, with especial orders to see that he had everything needful from the royal larder, but the servant forgot his charge when suddenly ordered to accompany the king to Woodstock.

St. Kenelm's Church is not far off the remains of Lord Lovel's house, whose name is spelt here as it appears in Shakespeare, though Minster Lovell has a double *l*, according to generally received spelling. This way of writing the name, however, is not imperative; for in the play of "Henry VIII.," which follows that of "Richard III.," Sir Thomas Lovell, a

Lancastrian, was a scion of this house, and his name is always spelt with a double *l*.

In the south transept of Minster Lovell Church is a figure of a knight in armour, with his feet resting on a dog; he was Lord Chamberlain of England in the reign of Edward III. Unless the blow has fallen more recently than the time when the notes were made for the present chapter, Minster Lovell Church has not suffered from the hands of the restorer. We may enjoy its antiquities and black oak pews in a way that leaves us grateful to the incumbent for letting well alone.

There was not a resident vicar of Minster Lovell for sixty years, the duties being performed by a curate from some neighbouring parish, and it may be partly owing to that that the church is in such fine old preservation. In the south transept is a monumental slab, which formed part of a monument in memory of Henry Heylyn, a colonel and commander in the army of Charles, and a nephew of Dr. Peter Heylyn. The latter-named gentleman took a farm at Minster Lovell in 1647, renting it from his nephew Henry. He lived six years here, and wrote many works—chiefly, however, his "Cosmographia." From this place he went to the pleasant town of Abingdon. While he resided at Minster Lovell he practised great hospitality, and his house was always open to distressed cavaliers. There is also a stone outside the south door with a coat-of-arms in memory of John Wheeler, who died in the year 1672; and Jane, his wife, a daughter of Thomas and Elizabeth Keble, who belonged to the family from which the poet descended. A reredos was erected in 1876 in memory of the late Lady Taunton, the widow of Elias Taunton, Knight, who possessed a large property here. This was designed, it seems, by Mr. Pearson, an eminent architect. There is much about Minster Lovell in the library of Lincoln Cathedral, which the curious will have little difficulty in obtaining access to.

One end of Wychwood Forest slopes down to Minster Lovell, and it yet bears the name of Minster Wood. It is bounded by Minster Ridings and Crawley Ridings, which circumstance has no other interest, perhaps, than as being an instance of the long lease old designations have in England.

A lonely walk, full of interest, would lead us to Cornbury Park, though, without some local knowledge, this is a difficult road to find even with an Ordnance map. Perhaps, however, this is not the most easy way of reaching Cornbury, though every road round Oxford is worth travelling along.

The road from the north lodge at Blenheim to Charlbury lies through a somewhat sterile country and the remains of old forest lands. If we take the northern road, it passes through King's Wood, Shire Wood, and Lee's Rest, till it reaches Cornbury Park, through which a path takes us to Wychwood Forest. A south road leads through the dreary villages of Stonesfield and Fawler, and passes a pleasantly-situated water-mill, almost adjoining the Oxford and Worcester railway.

Cornbury Park is the seat of Lord Churchill, and it was purchased for a branch of the Marlborough family that now has become ennobled. The house stands almost in the middle of an extensive park of great beauty. The views of it from Charlbury are delightful, especially from the churchyard. This park seems to have had many changes of owners and tenants, and many of them have left their names, if not their marks, in English history. Edward, Earl of Clarendon, lived here; and the estate at one time belonged to Henry Danvers,

Earl of Danby. Lord Leicester also, the husband of Amy Robsart, died here—it is said from a dose of poison.

One side of Cornbury is bounded by the ancient forest of Wychwood, which formerly was a royal hunting domain, but is now a wild tract, similar to many others round Oxford that have not been enclosed and farmed. There are some remains of forest left, and some coppices and heaths, intersected with roads. There are several ancient barrows in it, and Akeman Street, one of the grand Roman roads, runs through it. This forest covers about ten square miles, and is one of the sixty-eight that belonged to the royal families, and caused so much trouble in the times of the early kings. A recent historian remarks that at the period of the Conquest, at least a third of England was covered with woods or thickets or scrubs, and another third was heaths and moor, while in both east and west there were vast tracts of marsh-land; fens of nearly a hundred miles long severed East Anglia from the Eastern Counties. Beavers and wolves were abundant in the wilds, and London craftsmen hunted the wild ox in the woods of Hampstead. Some of the Roman roads even were grown over, though the principal ones, like Watling Street, were in use. Still, these had become little more than highways in the wilderness. The splendid civilisation that the Romans brought with them was not only gone, but it did not outlive their departure a day; the people were quite unprepared for it, and their masters took no pains to fit them. Thorns had come up in the palaces, and nettles and brambles in the fortifications; and as for their cities, the only inhabitants were the owl and the raven. Dr. Green points out that the forest laws were indirectly a proof that the prosperity of England was increasing, and the stag and wild ox were retreating before the woodman's axe. Wild animals have a forewarning of their fate; and one cause of the animosity that breaks out from time to time in the red man of the West towards his white neighbour is that he goes further and further away from the clearings in the woods.

It has sometimes been a matter of wonder that all the cities and palaces of the Romans should have disappeared so suddenly; but even after making allowance for all the clearing away of the materials which they were built of, allowance must be made for the rapidity with which the most cultivated land becomes wild with neglect. Draw a cordon round Blenheim Park, and let it be untrodden for fifty years only, and nearly every trace of garden will have disappeared. Decayed leaves would soon fill the walks and form a rich mould, and the weeds that have been fought down would soon re-assert their rule, while the finest of the garden flowers would seed and run wild, and long before the half-century was over those that had lived through the persecutions of the weeds would have resumed their original and more hardy type This, on a small scale, is only what England underwent on a large scale after the Romans left her; and it is more than probable that villas as beautiful as that at Northbeach lie under the roots of Wychwood Forest.

Here it is said Edward IV. first saw Elizabeth Woodville, who besought him to grant again the sequestered estates of her husband, and he became so enamoured with her beauty that he broke off a royal marriage and made her his wife; and what a picture she has left behind her of the unrest which in those days lay in store for the head that wore a crown! The wife of a king, the mother of two promising sons, who were murdered, and the mother of a queen, she died in imprisonment, to which she had been committed by her son-in-law.

Charlbury parish church is a fine old structure of various styles of architecture, and the living is of great value. It would almost be a pity when here not to go on to Spilsbury—pronounced Spal, Spel, Spil, &c., by the various inhabitants of whom you may ask the road, and who are sure delicately to correct your pronunciation by giving you something different in reply. All the vowels seem to be pressed into the service by the rustics. The hills are of remarkable beauty after leaving Charlbury, and the ivy-covered church is situated in a yard of amazing loveliness.

From Spilsbury to Ditchley the road lies through undulating lands; and there is much in the name of Ditchley that brings us back to the most stirring times in English history. Scott has immortalised the old knight; and whatever view any one may take of the particular merits of either side, one thing is sometimes almost overlooked when, as in the present age, we are apt to dive below the surface of things and view them from our own vantage-ground. Both of the factions—the supporters of Charles and of Cromwell—are entitled to our sincere admiration for the part they so gallantly took in fighting for what they thought was the right. A vast advance had been made upon the Wars of the Roses, and men for the moment seemed to have a measure of the freedom of choice. A spirit of inquiry was abroad, wrongs on one side or another were felt, and the men of England for a short time rose to the task of thinking for themselves. Perhaps in no great question has the courage and sense of duty been more conspicuously shown at any time since. Indeed, in reading the memoirs of the period the actual merits are quite lost sight of in a county history, though, indeed, the events of the wars form a considerable item in its pages. The siege of Latham House, Basing House, Oxford, and

KIDLINGTON.

Chester are monuments to the devotion of both sides; and the devotion of Sir Henry Lee is immortalised by Scott. "There is," he says, "a handsome parish church in the town of Woodstock. I am told so, at least, for I never saw it, having scarce time when at the place to view the magnificence of Blenheim, its painted halls and tapestried bowers, and then return in due season to dine in full with my learned friend the provost of ——; being one of those occasions on which a man wrongs himself extremely if he lets his curiosity interfere with his punctuality. I had the church accurately described to me, with a view to this work, but as I have some reason to doubt whether my informant had ever seen the inside of it himself, I shall be content to say that it is now a handsome edifice, most part of which was rebuilt forty or fifty years since, although it still contains some arches of the old chantry, founded, it is said, by King John. It is to this more ancient part of the building that my story refers;" and now, as has been said, it would not be possible to supply the want Sir Walter spoke of.

The picture of the times is so accurately drawn that it is quoted here even at length; and just the same scenes must have been common to every county in England.

"When the sermon was finished, the military orator wiped his brow, for notwithstanding the coolness of the weather, he was heated with the vehemence of his speech and action. He then descended from the pulpit, and spoke a word or two to the corporal who commanded the party of soldiers, who, replying by a sober nod of intelligence, drew his men together, and marched them in order to their quarters in the town.

"The preacher himself, as if nothing extraordinary had happened, left the church and sauntered through the streets of Woodstock, with the air of a stranger who was viewing the

town, without seeming to observe that he was himself, in his
turn, anxiously surveyed by the citizens, whose furtive yet
frequent glances seemed to regard him as something alike
suspected and dreadful, yet on no account to be provoked.   He
heeded them not, but stalked on in the manner affected by the
distinguished fanatics of the day—a stiff, solemn pace, a severe
and at the same time a contemplative look, like that of a man
discomposed at the interruption which earthly objects forced
upon him, obliging him by their intrusion to withdraw his
thoughts for an instant from celestial things.   Innocent pleasures of what kind soever they held in suspicion and contempt,
and innocent mirth they abominated.   It was, however, a cast
of mind that formed men for great and manly actions, as it
adopted principle, and that of an unselfish character, for the
ruling motive instead of the gratification of passion.   Some of
these men were indeed hypocrites, using the cloak of religion
only as a covering for their ambition ; but many really possessed the devotional character and the severe republican virtue,
which others only affected.   By far the greater number hovered
between these extremes—felt to a certain extent the power of religion, and complied with the times in affecting a great deal.   The
individual whose pretensions to sanctity, written as they were
upon his brow and gait, have given rise to the above digression,
reached at length the extremity of the principal street, which
terminates upon the park of Woodstock.   A battlemented
portal of Gothic appearance defended the entrance to the
avenue.   It was of mixed architecture, but on the whole,
though composed of the styles of the different ages when it had
received additions, had a striking and imposing effect.   An
immense gate, composed of rails of hammered iron, with many
a flourish and scroll, displaying as its uppermost ornament the

ill-fated cipher of ' C. R.,' was now decayed, being partly wasted with rust, partly by violence. The stranger paused, as if uncertain whether he should demand or essay entrance. He looked through the grating down an avenue skirted by majestic oaks, which led onward with a gentle curve as if into the depths of some ample and ancient forest. The wicket of the large iron gate being left unwittingly open, the soldier was tempted to enter, yet with some hesitation, as he that intrudes upon ground which he conjectures may be prohibited—indeed, his manner showed more reverence for the scene than could have been expected from his condition and character. He slackened his stately and consequential pace, and at length stood still and looked around him.

"Not far from the gate he saw rising from the trees one or two ancient and venerable turrets, bearing each its own vane of rare device, glittering in the autumn sun. These indicated the ancient hunting-seat, or lodge, as it was called, which had, since the time of Henry II., been occasionally the residence of the English monarchs when it pleased them to visit the woods of Oxford, which then so abounded with game that, according to old Fuller, huntsmen and falconers were nowhere better pleased. The situation which the lodge occupied was a piece of flat ground, now planted with sycamores, not far from the entrance of that magnificent spot where the spectator first stops to gaze upon Blenheim, to think of Marlborough's victories, and to applaud or criticise the cumbrous magnificence of Vanbrugh's style.

"There, too, paused our military preacher, but with other thoughts and for other purpose than to admire the scene around him. It was not long afterwards when he beheld two persons —a male and female—approaching slowly, and so deeply engaged in their own conversation that they did not raise their eyes to observe that there stood a stranger in the path before them. The soldier took advantage of their state of abstraction, and desirous at once to watch their motions and avoid their observation, he glided beneath one of the huge trees which skirted the path, and whose boughs, sweeping the ground on every side, insured him against discovery, unless in case of actual search.

" In the meantime, the gentleman and lady continued to advance, directing their course to a rustic seat, which still enjoyed the sunbeams, and was placed adjacent to the tree where the stranger was concealed.

" The man was elderly, yet seemed bent more by sorrows and infirmity than by the weight of years. He wore a mourning cloak over a dress of the same melancholy colour, cut in that picturesque form which Vandyck has rendered immortal. But although the dress was handsome, it was put on and worn with a carelessness which showed the mind of the wearer ill at ease. His aged yet still handsome countenance had the same air of consequence which distinguished his dress and his gait; a striking part of his appearance was a long white beard, which descended far over the breast of his slashed doublet, and looked singular from its contrast in colour with his habit."

The Commission sitting on ancient manuscripts have published some very interesting documents from Ditchley, though they say they are not numerous. They consist, among other things, of a large folio volume, which contains Wycliffe's translation of the Gospels of St. Matthew and St. Mark, with commentaries in English. Mr. Macray, of Oxford, has placed a note in the volume which may be adopted here. He says the version of the Gospels is the earlier of the two Wycliffite versions issued about 1380. In some parts, however, it has words that occur in the later version; and the commentaries in this book are of peculiar interest and value. That on Matthew is in other versions, but the interest in this particular copy is that it contains passages of great length copied from Grosteste, condemning the abuses of the Papal system; and these, as far as Mr. Macray is aware, do not appear in other copies. The commentary on Mark is unknown, and not mentioned in Shirley's list of Wycliffe's works.

There are here some interesting letters of the Stuarts, but not of political value. Charles II. had a peculiar taste for horse-racing, and, in a letter to his daughter, the Countess of Lichfield, says he is going to Newmarket, where he has "much business." And there is also here an original letter from Lord Chancellor Jeffreys, announcing the birth of a son, in the year 1688, to the king and queen. This child it was that cost James II. his throne; for it was understood that he would be brought up a Papist, and so the Romish religion perpetuated. Singularly enough, also, it was very generally discredited at the time. When Sir Henry Lee lived, Ditchley was described as a low timber house, with a pretty bowling-green; now it is a large stone mansion designed by Gibbs.

There is in the house a portrait of Sir Henry Lee and his dog, the celebrated Bevis, who lay all night, it is said, under his bed on one occasion, and could not be driven away, though his master had never made a pet of him, but at midnight, when he was asleep, a servant quietly entered the room to murder him, and the dog sprang out upon him. Sir Henry awoke, and the man was captured.

The tale is quite within the bounds of probability, for there is abundant reason to believe that dogs understand much that is said in ordinary conversation. When a dog is old and infirm he is often destroyed; and there are authenticated instances, that when it has been spoken of, the dog whose days were to be cut short has left the house and never returned.

From Ditchley there is a road back to Oxford through Woodstock, Begbrook, and Wolvercot, but parts of this road are rather dreary. A much more pleasant way, and not more than a couple of miles farther, is through Glympton and past Shipton, then through Woodstock Road station, leaving Kidlington on the left, and so entering Oxford through Summerstown.

Kidlington is well worth a visit; the trees round the church are of great beauty, and the church is an excellent specimen of Decorated architecture; it has been built apparently about the year 1350. The village also is very delightful, and reminds one of some of the French hamlets, with its paved streets, high walls, and roomy houses. The church is at the end of the village, and a rustic pathway through fields leads past Hampton Poyle, and on to Bletchington; this road crosses the Cherwell, where there is a rope ferry.

Kidlington formerly belonged to Robert D'Oilley, whose great-uncle came over to England in the train of William the Conqueror, and he give this church, with some others and extensive grants of lands, to Osney Abbey. But it has rather a special interest to the student of the old monasteries, for in the twenty-seventh of King Henry VIII. Dr. William Petre was rewarded with the gift in fee of the advowsons of Kidlington, Merton, and Yarnton, Oxon; and Long Wittenham, Berks; which he afterwards annexed to Exeter College, Oxford. These grants he obtained in consequence of his energy in the commission he received from Cromwell, to repair to all the

KIDLINGTON CHURCH.

monasteries and make inquiry into the government and be-
haviour of both sexes—a commission that he executed with
exceeding violence and scurrility.   The sacrament of the mass
was held sacred by the general body of Englishmen ; but
soon after Dr. Petre had been on his mission it was openly
derided.   Transubstantiation, which as yet was recognised by
law, was held up to scorn in ballads and mystery plays ; and
on one occasion, when the priest was elevating the host, a
lawyer raised his dog up.   Even the parts which had always
been regarded with most solemnity, such as the consecration,
" hoc est corpus," were travestied into a nickname for jugglery,
" hocus pocus," until Henry himself became weary of such
doings, and there was a reaction in favour of the old religion
that went so far as to revive persecution, and burning was
the punishment for those who denied transubstantiation.

The Decorated windows at Kidlington are of the late
flowing kind, and very well proportioned.   The tracery is
common in this style, and indicates the latter part of the
fourteenth century.   It is formed, as will be seen, by the
mullions parting fram each other when they join at the top of
the lights, and separating and then joining again.

But another trip, and one of less formidable length, is to
leave Oxford by the Summerstown Road ; and exactly at the
fourth milestone there is a footpath road that leads to Kidlington, and passing through the village the other one is almost in
a line with this.   Woodstock Road station and Kirtlington are
convenient for pedestrians in this locality.   And here we can
cross over to Marston, a very old-fashioned village, and containing the church, shown here.   It would seem to have been
built about the year 1500, though I have no records at hand
to indicate the precise date of the masonry.   There is a pond

on one side in which there is often a curiously clear reflection of the church. The gift of the living of Marston is in the Whorwood family.

In Marston, Skelton says, was the " residence of Unton Croke, Esq., and he acquired it this marriage." The house was made use of by the king, and the army of the Parliamentarians, in the treaty which they drew up for the surrender of the City of Oxford, after it was compelled to give up the contest, took possession of it, and then it was converted into a post-house for the village. There are in the church several interesting monuments of the Croke family, and the inscriptions upon these are given in Sir Alexander Croke's genealogical table of his ancestry. The Crokes still have large possessions in Oxfordshire, and are among the oldest families in the kingdom. They are descended from the Counts of Guisnes, who counted among their progenitors Emperors and Kings of France, Counts of Flanders, and Dukes of Bavaria. Formerly the name was Blount, and members of this family continually appear in English history, always with credit and distinction. Sir Thomas Blount endeavoured to restore Richard II. to the throne, and was put to death with nameless barbarity. When in the agonies of death, the King's Chamberlain said, " Go seek a master that can cure thee ; " and Blount only answered, " ' Te deum laudamus.' Blessed is the day on which I was born, and blessed be this day, for I shall die in the service of my sovereign lord the noble King Richard." Nicholas le Blount then fled to Italy and entered the service of Visconti, accompanied by others who had been compromised in the attempt ; and as Visconti was at war with the Emperor, they found congenial work, and drove the Emperor out of Italy. A number of them returned then to England, but took the

MARSTON CHURCH.

precaution of changing their names, Nicholas le Blount
assuming that of Croke. Sir John Croke, in Queen Elizabeth's
time, succeeded Sir Edward Coke as Treasurer of the Inner
Temple, and was Recorder of London. Sir George Croke, in
Charles I.'s time, was one of the judges of King's Bench.
He continually uttered his protest against the unconstitutional
proceedings he saw going on round him, and, undismayed by
threats as he was proof against the fascinations of power, he
always raised his voice in favour of the rights of the people.
In the celebrated case of Hampden, when five judges had
decided for the Crown, Justice Croke delivered his opinion
very decidedly in favour of the great patriot.

CHAPTER IX.

"This castle hath a pleasant seat; the air
Nimbly and sweetly recommends itself
Unto our gentle senses."—*Macbeth*.

Old Woodstock—Palace Sold—Ancient Roof there—Chaucer resides at Woodstock—
Henry III.—Woodstock Old Church—Georgian Church Architecture—Old Woodstock
restored—Blenheim—Sir John Vanbrugh and his Works—Introduces a Peculiar Style
--Waagen on Blenheim—Hearne—Spence—Thackeray on Blenheim.

BOW WINDOW, MAGDALEN.

THE town of Woodstock is said to have been the birthplace of Chaucer, the poet, as it was long his residence. Warton, in his "History of English Poetry," tells us that he procured a painting of Chaucer on a panel from an old quadrangular house in Woodstock, where it had been preserved; the last remains of this house, including a panelled room with a carved oak roof, called Chaucer's bed-chamber, were demolished about twenty-five years before Warton's work appeared. Geoffrey Chaucer espoused Philippa, daughter and co-heir of Sir Payne Holt, of Hainault, one of the maids of honour to Queen Philippa. She was the sister of the wife of John of Gaunt, which may in some measure account for the attachment between him and Chaucer.

Kennet says that Henry VII. added greatly to the beauty of the buildings of Woodstock, particularly the front gate and principal entrance. On it was his name and an English rhyme importing that he was the founder; and in this gatehouse it is said that the Princess (afterwards Queen) Elizabeth was imprisoned. The apartment in which she lodged remained complete nearly until Warton's time, and retained a magnificent roof carved out of Irish oak, and was called until its destruction "Queen Elizabeth's Room."

Woodstock Palace suffered during the Great Rebellion, and the old furniture of the palace was sold, while Cromwell apportioned the building to three of his followers. Two of them pulled down the building for the sake of the stones, and the third part, in which was the gatehouse, fell into the hands of Lord Lovelace, who converted it into his dwelling. Sir John Vanbrugh had the taste to preserve it, and spent £2,000 in keeping the ruins of the pile from desecration; and old persons living in Warton's time could remember a gorgeous porch and chapel windows of great magnificence; but the Lord Treasurer Godolphin, who afterwards married the Duke of Marlborough's eldest daughter, remarked to his mother-in-law that such a building was not fit for the eyes of Sarah Jennings, and in a moment an order was given for the destruction of one of the most interesting buildings in England : one compared with which Blenheim in all its glory would be considered by many to have hardly any value at all.

There is a curious document relating to old Woodstock among the historic documents which the Royal Commission has found with many others belonging to the Corporation of Bridgewater—the petition of a carpenter to the king—probably Henry VII. ; and he subscribes himself " from your poure

and faithful subject, your carpenter, John Bricine." The
plea is one which any court now (if it is properly set forth—
and it has very much the appearance of being so) would allow.
He says that he showed the king what the nature of the roof
was to be, and gave him a "sight by picture." This, of course,
alludes to a plan and section, and he reminds the king that
he was "content according to the said plan." After, however,
he had proceeded to a considerable extent with his work, he
was stopped, and the Prior of Llantony showed the carpenter
how the roof was to be "transposed otherwise." A "round
window" appears to have been in some manner in the way,
which seems rather curious, because circular windows belonged
to an earlier period, and it must have been there before the
work was commenced or when the king had a sight of the
picture. But the poor carpenter plaintively declares that part
of his timber was used at the offices of Woodstock, and part of
it was appropriated by other carpenters, and unless he receives
ıx*li*. he will be unable to complete the second roof. He finishes
his seemingly reasonable request in the following words:—
"And Allmyghte Jesu preserve your Majeste royall, long to
prosper and endure." How many times the sum he asks
the king for would he now get for his roof? An excursion in
1634 speaks of this hall as being "church-like, with aisles,
and pillars, and rich tapestry hangings." The same excursion also speaks of a furious wild boar having just been
killed in the neighbouring woods. Drayton's account of
Rosamond's labyrinth corresponds with one that appears
in this excursion; and he says that her "well being paved
with square stones at the bottom, and also her bower from
which the labyrinth did run, are yet remaining, being vaults
arched with stone and brick, almost inextricably wound one

within the other, by which, if her lodging were laid about by the Queene, she might easily avoid peril imminent, and, if needs be, by scant issues take the air abroad, many furlongs from Woodstock, in Oxfordshire."

It is not certain that the commonly-received accounts of Chaucer's natal place having been at Woodstock is correct, but he spent much time here, and such details can hardly have much value beyond curiosity. We pass a broad, old-fashioned mansion in Liverpool that has the quiet air of the residence of a man of wealth of the last century, and this was the natal place of one of the most prominent statesmen of our times; and I often think (if such details are of value) that had he been born a few centuries since, half a dozen dwellings, from a castle in Scotland or one in Wales, to a hall near Seaforth, would have been definitely pointed out by various historians as the real spot, and perhaps plenty of letters, confirming the various theories, adduced in testimony. This would not have been alluded to, but that I just saw the question discussed in a leading local paper; and the statesman spoken of is not only alive, but hardly advanced in years.

The influence of such men as Chaucer is of much more importance than their birthplace; for, as has been said—"The largeness of heart, the wide tolerance which enables him to reflect man for us as none but Shakespeare has ever reflected it, but to reflect it with a pathos, a shrewd sense, and kindly humour, a freshness and joyousness of feeling, that even Shakespeare has not surpassed."

He it was that first induced Englishmen to estimate the value of "pardons hot from Rome;" and he did much to stir up his countrymen to resist the great authority the Pope held here. For in Chaucer's life-time the Pope drew, it is

generally believed, five times as great a revenue out of England
as the king himself did.

Hardly any trace remains of old Woodstock. There is a
curious chimney-shaft, apparently of the latter part of the

OLD REMAINS AT WOODSTOCK.

fourteenth century, which, tradition—of course, in this instance
inaccurately—says, was on the residence of the Black Prince.
Parliaments were held at Woodstock; and, according to
generally received accounts, a royal marriage was celebrated
at Woodstock.

Henry III. held several courts at Woodstock. It would

appear that some rather important events took place in connection with some of these; but his many years of misgovernment had made him obnoxious to every class in England. His expenditure exceeded his revenues by ever so much, and abbeys and sees were kept vacant for purposes of extortion. It is said that a Romish priest, Ribaud, attempted his life here, and he was taken to Oxford and quartered. There is hardly a doubt that he was some ecclesiastic; that if we could hear his tale now, it would show much, not, it is true, to excuse his shameful crime, but to explain how he became distracted with a list of wrongs. A guide-book to Oxford says that John built a chapel for the portion of the town known as New Woodstock, and it is said a portion of it is now standing. I have no hesitation in saying that I think the report extremely likely; but this must remain a matter of speculation. For ever since commencing this work I had hoped to have been able to give one or two illustrations of Woodstock Church; part of it was comparatively new, but some of it must have been moss-grown even in Fair Rosamond's time. The new parts were quite old enough to be interesting; they belonged to the Georgian period, and might have been nearly contemporaneous with Blenheim; perhaps they were: at any rate, the style was very much the same.

And here I must say one word for Georgian architecture in churches, including the "pew system," as it is called. By the "pew system" is understood the renting of a pew with a door, or having a pew where we can go to. These pews are not always rented: they may belong to a house or a farm; and some not unpleasant interiors have been painted by Nash and Prout, of square oak pews, with a lion, or a porcupine, or any family emblem, cut or emblazoned on the doors, and forming a strong Vandyck-brown foreground. The early Georgian period, and perhaps half a century before that, was the time when these were best understood; and precious indeed oak pews of the earlier Georgian period are becoming in any parish church.   How superior they are to modern open benches !   The open benches that have taken the place of pews are so very like market-stalls, without the baskets of mackerel or whiting to give them life and colour.   Besides this, I have more than once been in a church where fine old black oak pews were swept away for modern free benches, and in my innocence had supposed that the freedom was real—as real as it is in a cathedral, for subscriptions had been invited on those grounds; but I saw persons as unsophisticated as myself politely asked to leave their seats because some retired tradesman or half-pay colonel had appropriated them, and would soon be in the building—residents, of course—and each, in their measure, subscribers for the "restoration."   Well, during the month of July I saw this church at Woodstock, but, unhappily, left making sketches of it till a future visit.   An ominous begging-box, with a lock, stood out in the street, asking for funds for the "restoration."   One would have thought it almost a burlesque, for it wanted no restoration at all, and would have lasted for ever so many centuries; but the box was put up by those "who had said in their hearts, Let us make havoc of it altogether."   Within a few weeks of the time this interesting monument was perfect, not one beam was left ; and now, as I write, it is a "heap of stones."   Through the *débris* I could just distinguish a fine old Norman doorway that has survived ever so many scenes notable in history, but it was nearly covered up with ruins; and supposing that it does escape the general *mêlée*, and has the luck to be inserted in a new church, with open benches and modern adornments, it will have lost every claim to interest, and be scraped down by unloving hands to appear like a new doorway. Happily, though rather late in the day, an end is approaching to these vandalisms. A Government Commission for the preservation of old monuments has been appointed, and, what is of even more importance, a voluntary society has sprung up for the preservation of old churches and abbey buildings. The answer to any cleric who thinks that his church is crumbling, and who justly asks, " What shall I do?" is very clear—" Probably you are mistaken; but, at any rate, do not consult a professional church restorer; go to a first-class, intelligent builder, and ask him what is really wanted to secure its stability. The church restorer will do just the same in the first instance, and you will see him go round the building with a very unpretending-looking person, talking low, but earnestly; then the unpretending-looking person will disappear from the scene, and you will have a ' practical ' report in some days, and ' after much consideration ' from the church restorer."

Now, if a builder is employed to secure stability, that is all that is wanted at present, for certainly before this century is over there will be a new class of architects, who really understand church preservation, and will leave a grand old front as they find it, or without it being known that a restorer was ever at work.

I have just been to see some extremely fine early sixteenth century woodwork in a cathedral. It often struck me as being without any superior in England for dignity and beauty; and its colour was a deep Vandyck-brown, with just a slight tinge of purple. A restoring architect, a " fashionable one from London," as they said, had been called in to restore it, and this he did by scraping and sand-papering it to appear new, cutting out, according to his desire, the excellent carved work, and breaking it down with axes and hammers. Now, it is only the work of yesterday, and not a tint has been added to tone its ghastly paleness.

With what delight do I find in the *Builder* of June 30th, 1866, a notice of a real restorer—one who is worthy the name; and how willingly do I transcribe it :—

" Mr. G. A. Rogers has restored some of the carvings which were executed for the Galton estate of Lord Monson, and are attributed to Gibbons. These fine works (like many others of the same period) have been attacked and all but destroyed by the destructive agency of worms and beetles. Mr. Rogers has, however, with great care restored these works to almost their original strength and beauty. Firstly, he had them photographed, then he took the carvings to pieces, and thoroughly destroyed every germ of insect life by means of corrosive sublimate and other poisons. This done, the rotten portions were scraped out from the back (*which in most cases were reduced to fine powder*), and then the cavities thus made were filled up with a soft, hardening substance. The next operation was to fill up the innumerable worm-holes in the front surface, remount the carvings by aid of the photographs, and varnish the wood to equalise the colour. A specimen of the carving, retained in its decayed state, shows how far the carvings were decayed, and contrasts remarkably with the finished frame." All honour to Mr. Rogers! How is it that, among all the destruction that has impoverished the land, his name is not a household word? If those that have done such wrong prosper in the world and have riches in possession, he ought to be high up in the peerage; many a title has been conferred for half such a service as he has rendered, even among those that have been rightly granted. Yet this scientific treatment would apply not

only to wood, but to stone.   I took the freedom of italicising
some of the words, which do not appear so in the *Builder ;*
but these show the real difficulties he had to contend with ;
and I say without hesitation, that not one single restoring
architect of those who have made restoration their practice
would have scrupled unhesitatingly to condemn the wood as
worthless and quite impracticable.

One remark it is hardly possible to avoid here, and that is,
that whenever a new stone or enrichment is inserted into an
old tower or front, it is nearly certain that it will be left in
its original tint, and no effort made to harmonise it with the
surrounding masonry. This, at any rate, does not proceed from
the love of destruction, but simply shows how far the modern
architects are from appreciating what belongs to the picturesque.
Because if we suppose, for the sake of argument and at the expense of history, that it was necessary to remove the ancient
enrichment and substitute a new one, a few shillings, or pence
even, would have made all the difference.   It is hardly to be
supposed that any professional man would confuse this finish
with Ruskin's excellent remarks on shams.   The argument
of the Hibernian, who preferred a tear to a patch in a garment,
on the grounds that one showed poverty and the other might
be the accident of the day, was sound and philosophical in
comparison ; and it would be only in keeping with the architect,
if this is really the cause of his employing untinted stone, to
recommend any patch a garment might require (and accidents
will happen to those only a day old) to be inserted in undyed
cloth, for fear of falling under Ruskin's just strictures on shams.
Nobody would think of tinting a new building to look like an
old one, except perhaps the proprietor of a tea-garden ; but to
insert a hard new stone to do duty in a time-stained building

shows the work of unloving hands.   There is not the slightest
desire to intimate here that the new church at Woodstock may
not be an excellent piece of modern architecture—it is quite in
probability that it may be so: nothing at all connected with the
circumstances would induce me to intimate the contrary; but
it simply displaces a pile of interest, and if it preserves the
ancient parts at all, does so at the cost of all their value.

Blenheim, it is not necessary to say, was the work of Sir
John Vanbrugh, who was the architect of perhaps more
country mansions of consequence than any other man.   A
representative of his family, and the last of the line, died
comparatively recently near Liverpool.   He was a gentleman
of affluence, inherited in part, it is said, from the labours of
his well-known predecessor, and he held the valuable living
of Aughton, near Ormskirk, till his death.   Perhaps Pope's
sneer at Sir John—

> "Lie heavy on him, earth, for he
> Laid many a heavy weight on thee"—

is hardly deserved.   In fact, he himself afterwards regretted it,
and admitted its injustice, and said that at any rate it was
written of a man of integrity and honour.

Sir John Vanbrugh was the grandson of a Hollander who
fled from the persecutions of the Duke of Alva.   His son became a sugar-refiner in Chester, and succeeded in amassing a
large fortune, and after this he returned to London, and became
the Comptroller of the Treasury Chamber.   He married the
youngest daughter and co-heir of Sir Dudley Carleton, a gentleman of Surrey, and Sir John was the second son of their issue.
He was not always intended for the profession of architecture,
but was in the first instance sent to France to learn the
military art, and here he imbibed many French ideas of art

which appear conspicuously in his works; but he soon returned, and was appointed a commissioner of Greenwich Hospital—converting it into a hospital from a palace. But like his contemporary, Mason, he had many accomplishments outside his profession, and was one of the favourite writers of comic dramas in England. He and Congreve may be said to have divided the honours of the comic muse of the period between them, though perhaps their compositions are little read in the present day, when we have an abundance of literature so much more desirable and amusing. Vanbrugh succeeded in erecting the old theatre in the Haymarket, which was afterwards converted into an opera-house, and he and his friend Congreve managed it jointly; but Congreve retired, and Vanbrugh then took the entire control upon himself. Singularly enough, we do not know at what time he became an architect. Blenheim is commonly alluded to as his greatest work, but many prefer Castle Howard, in Yorkshire, the seat of the Earl of Carlisle. He was also the architect for Eastbury, the seat of Bubb Dodington; Easton Weston; Eaton Hall, near Chester, now enlarged into a building of very much greater dimensions than Blenheim, and although only a small part of it remains exposed, the old building is almost completely embedded in the new one. According to a painting that remains at Eaton, however, it must have been a stately edifice, built of Dutch brick, with stone dressings, and not very like his usual style. In judging of Italian architecture in this country, we must always recollect the difficulties that the designers had to contend with. The rooms of the buildings required to be lower and the light greater than in the prototypes in Italy; and Vanbrugh, who lived for some time on the Continent, had to overcome some of his early training to adapt himself to the requirements of his

employers. But he almost seems to have failed in grasping
the means at his hand, or perhaps, to speak more truly,
these were kept in check by the quasi-classic lore and devices
of the age.

Italy was the great centre of the arts in the Middle Ages.
Dante, Petrarch, and Boccaccio may almost be said to have
struck off the fetters from free thought, and in due time we
have three schools of architecture and art—the Roman, the
Florentine, and the Venetian, founded, one may almost say, by
Bramante, Brunelleschi, and San Michele. The Venetian style
may be said to have adapted ancient architecture to modern wants,
and the works of San Michele and Sansovino quite bent the
ancient forms to modern uses. Palladio was the great disciple
of this school, and perhaps advanced it to its highest excellence.
The three, however, soon lost their distinguishing features and
merged into one. It spread over Europe; and Spain, France,
and England each adapted to it some characteristic features of
their own. In France it became the singular style which is
called the Louis Quatorze, and more singular style called Louis
Quinze, or Rococo—which, indeed, was little more than a
debasement of its predecessor. This Louis Quatorze style
found imitators in England in our own Carolean; and when
Anne came to the throne architecture was at a low ebb, and
everything in the shape of British art frowned down. Everything was artificial and stilted. Beaux and belles wore hair-
powder; toes were pointed out in walking, as being the most
unnatural method of progression that was at all practicable;
and the head-dresses the ladies wore would have made even
the fashions of modern days look spiritless; while the heels
of their boots raised them above the level of the ground
higher than a laundress's pattens; and unaccountable pieces

BLENHEIM PALACE, FROM THE LAKE.

of sticking-plaister were pasted over their faces, cut out in every eccentric form they could invent. Perhaps they had no object other than the pleasure of revelling in grossness of taste; and if the navigators of the day had brought over a tattooer from the Pacific Islands, they would in all human probability have realised immense fortunes by setting up shops near Covent Garden. There was no National Gallery, no British Museum, no Royal Academy, and the portrait painters were imported from abroad. The wonder, indeed, is that such men as Wren and Vanbrugh could find any encouragement at all.

As for the particular merits of Blenheim, it may be well to give two quotations. One is the enthusiastic account of Waagen, sometime director of the Royal Gallery of Berlin, and he says :—

"After I had spent a day and a half at Oxford, I proceeded to Blenheim, the celebrated country seat of the Duke of Marlborough. If nothing were to be seen in England but this seat, with its park and treasures of art, there would be no reason to repent the journey to this country. The whole is on so grand a scale, that no prince in the world would need to be ashamed of it; and, at the same time, it is a noble monument of the gratitude of the English nation to the great Duke of Marlborough. It would be superfluous to add anything respecting the park." Side by side with this eulogy it may be as well to quote the synopsis of the able antiquary, Hearne; though some little allowance may be made for his ruffled feelings at the loss of a building in which he took such rapturous delight as Woodstock old palace.

"I walked this day (May 29) to Woodstock, and viewed the old ruins about Rosamond's Well, in Woodstock Park. There are the ruins of the labyrinth for Rosamond. This

labyrinth was a vast thing.   It joyned with the Palace.   The
workmen say that the old palace and the ruins of the
labyrinth exceed the foundations of the present Blenheim
House.   So they may very well conclude that the old palace
was a bigger thing than Blenheim House.   I never was in it
before.   It is grand; but a sad, irregular, confused piece of
work.   The architect (if a blockhead may deserve that name)
was Vanbrugg.   The hall is noble.   The painting of the top
was done by Thornehill.   It represents Marlborough's victory
at Blenheim.   There is one room in which lye some antiquities.
There are two bustos in it and two Moors.   But the greatest
piece of antiquity I saw in it is of white marble, like your
Parian marble, in which are several figures of Pleasure by a
river.   The Duke of Marlborough's misses are represented in
figures (by way of statues) on one side of the front of the house.
The new bridge (which hath cost £30,000) over the rivulet
below the house is wonderful : particularly upon account of the
arch—the biggest, at least one of the biggest, in the world—
and a show of antiquity.   This arch is 103 yards.   Went into
the gardens.   The garden of pleasure containes threescore acres;
the kitchen garden containes seven acres.   These gardens are
fine, and indeed exceed (if we consider things as anything perfect) the house, in which we have nothing convenient, most of
the rooms being small, pitifull, dark things.   By this work we
sufficiently see the genius of Vanbrugg."   Between these estimates there is of course a wide difference ; and those who are
interested may compare them or find a different mode of
criticism.   There can be no doubt that in the view shown the
palace stands well, and in a good aspect for the general effect of
light and shade it has to occupy in the landscape.   The semi-
circular, or, correctly speaking, segmental point, always has a

pleasing, hospitable effect, and was much in vogue in the early part of the eighteenth century. There was generally a colonnade, and sometimes these spreading wings were cut up into servants' offices. It may be well here to remark what has often struck me as of importance in a pair of gates in a lane which lead to a house. When these are set off with trees' they may be very pleasing and picturesque; but sometimes they have a stunted look, and the reason is not very far to seek. A gate to a park, whether it is in connection with a lodge or simply an entrance, should stand back from the road, and the wall or fence be curved in; this is generally the case, however. But the success of the entrance lies almost entirely in the form in which the wall is curved. In many recent gateways the wall ends on each side in a convex segment, and the gate is cramped in between them. Sometimes this convex segment is exchanged for an ogee, which hardly mends matters. The same forbidding look prevails. The right form for this opening is a single segment, with the gate in the middle. This has a liberal, hospitable look, and if it sacrifices a few feet of land from the park or grounds it is compensated for a hundred times over by the appearance. In other words, we may make a small plan of what I have endeavoured to describe by supposing the edge of a card to represent the wall, and then, if you take a snip out with an old-fashioned wad-cutter, that gives the form.

Vanbrugh was not equal in ability to Wren or Jones, and there is often a baldness in his details. The front of Blenheim, when we approach it, is singularly bare, though, judging from the park, we should not have expected to find it so. Wren sometimes, under compulsion, attempted mediæval architecture, as we see in the western towers of Westminster Abbey; though what he would have done if left free to act we may judge, it has been observed, from the work of Jones at St. Paul's. He added an elaborate Corinthian portico to the noble old church, and greatly desired to pull the ancient building down altogether, so that we have a debt of gratitude to some unknown friend for preserving the Abbey, and staying Sir Christopher. Now, it must always be recorded to the honour of Vanbrugh, that he tried to preserve the old palace of Woodstock, or, at least, the marvellous remains of it, and, as we have seen, he did succeed in doing so; and in all probability it would to this day have enriched the nation if some one had not, in an evil hour, pointed out that it was an unbecoming object for the eyes of Sarah Jennings to rest upon.

Two critiques of Blenheim have been already quoted, and there are two more that it is tempting to produce, so that a reasonable number of critics can be heard, and at least one's own responsibility shifted: for Blenheim is so important that it ought to occupy a considerable space in these pages.

Lending-libraries are now so common that it is not too much to say that nearly every person in England has access to one of them, and if his taste lies in reading travels or adventures, he will not do amiss if he searches a catalogue for those of the beginning of the present century or the end of the last. If it comes to reading Camden or Froissart, we expect to find things very different from scenes we are familiar with. But when we are so near the time we stand aghast at the changes steam and telegraphs have made in our island and the world. The librarian who lent the book which is before me narrated a journey by coach to London, when the up mail met the down one, on which he was a passenger, and some one connected with the service shouted out, at the top of his voice, " The king is

dead!" Now King William only died in the year 1837, yet
the news was unknown in Liverpool, and would be for twelve
hours; and when it might reach the Highlands of Scotland, say
Oban or Balmoral, one would hardly like to speculate. Yet hourly
news of any illness of the President of the United States or the
Viceroy of India is looked for as a matter of course. Mr. E. J.
Spence, writing in 1809 an account of his travels in England,
says that he hopes the various scenes and the habits of the
people in the counties he has explored will enable the reader to
"decide what town or county he should prefer as a residence,"
or "suggest to the tradesman or merchant where he is most
likely to extend his business." His letters speak of the entrance
to Oxford by moonlight, "which gave it a very sublime appearance, and cast a solemn grandeur on its magnificent edifices
rising in proud state one above another." The "Star Inn" is,
he says, "very fashionable indeed, but very expensive, noisy,
and disagreeable. A singular custom prevails in this house—
that is, playing on the harp every evening in the hall for the
entertainment of the company." But his account of Blenheim
is very much like the previous ones. "We came afterwards to
a high lodge, and at the distance of half a mile to an opening
in the woods, through which we beheld the palace of Blenheim,
finely seated on an eminence, with a noble lake winding through
a richly-wooded valley. A stately bridge, resembling the
Rialto at Venice, and the small picturesque town of Woodstock,
with its 'shady paths and verdant groves,' contribute to give
animation to the scene. The lake, which is a quarter of a mile
in breadth and a mile in length, is an artificial piece of water,
and derives all its beauty from Capability Brown." How
widely the bridge differs from the Rialto the photographs and
prints which excursionists bring back with them in abundance

nowadays will tell every one. But it seems almost strange that in taking leave of Blenheim he should in those days have taken exception to its stateliness. "Blenheim, notwithstanding its magnificence, will seldom, in my opinion, excite admiration: there is such a heavy pomp in its appearance. It is more fitted for a palace of state than a mansion to dwell in, as there is not a single apartment which has the least air of comfort." It may be remarked here, *en passant*, that our author, on September 4, 1809, went to Manchester Theatre, "to witness Mrs. Siddons' performance of Lady Macbeth, with the after-piece of 'Catherine and Petruchio,' in which she was to perform Catherine for her own benefit;" but he says that, as an example of the "prudent economy" of the men of Manchester, Mrs. Siddons, then in her youth, only realised seven shillings in sharing the results of her labour with the manager of the theatre. However, the noticeable part of Mr. Spence's estimate of Blenheim is the way in which it coincides with Thackeray's; for it is well known that his tremendous description of Castle Carabas has reference to this building, and is only slightly altered for obvious reasons. "At the entrance to the park there are a pair of great, gaunt, mildewed lodges—mouldy Doric temples— with black chimney-pots in the finest classic taste, and the gates of course are surmounted with *chats bottés*, the well-known supporters of the Carabas family . . . The gates were passed. A damp green stretch of park spread right and left immeasurably, confined by a chilly grey wall; and a damp, long, straight road, between two huge rows of most dismal lime-trees, leads up to the castle. In the midst of the park is a great black tank or lake, bristling over with rushes, and here and there covered with patches of pea-soup. A shabby temple rises on an island in this delectable lake, which is approached by a rotten barge that lies at roost in a dilapidated boat-house. Clumps of elms and oaks dot over the huge green flat. . . . I forgot to say the house is full in view all the way, except when intercepted by the trees on the miserable island in the lake—an enormous red-brick mansion, square, vast, and dingy.

"It is flanked by four stone towers with weathercocks. In the midst of the grand façade is a huge Ionic portico, approached by a vast, lonely, ghastly staircase. Rows of black windows framed in stone stretch out on either side right and left—three storeys, and eighteen windows of a row. You may see a picture of the palace and staircase in the views of England and Wales, with four carved and gilt carriages waiting on the gravel-walk, and several parties of ladies and gentlemen in wigs and hoops dotting the fatiguing lines of the stairs. . . . But these stairs are made in great houses for people *not* to ascend. The first Lady Carabas would be wet to the skin, if she got out of her gilt coach in a shower, before she got half-way up to the carved Ionic portico, where four dreary statues of Peace, Plenty, Piety, and Patriotism are the only sentinels;" and after a merciless description of the apartments, Thackeray concludes: "A single family has no more right to build itself a temple of that sort than to erect a Tower of Babel. It would require two thousand footmen to make the place cheerful."

In the face of such a scathing condemnation of the pile as this, it is pleasant to remember some agreeable scenes that many will think deserve kindlier treatment, though, probably, the general voice of the nation is with the great moralist.

Still, it must always be remembered that he was never very kindly disposed to the owners of Blenheim, for, not only in the series from which the above extract is taken, but in other of Thackeray's works, the family are painted in not pleasant colours. Witness, for example, in "Vanity Fair," the flight from Brussels on the eve of Waterloo, when, in his covered satire, he tells how the family fled in confusion in their carriage from the approach of the French, as indeed they might be well excused for doing under the circumstances in which he placed them.

WATERFALL, BLENHEIM.

CHAPTER X.

"Are not these woods
More free from peril than the envious court?
Here feel we but the penalty of Adam,
The seasons' difference."—*As You Like It*.

Trees at Blenheim—Titian Gallery—Blenheim Collection—Strafford—Smallness of Ruins at Blenheim—Lake and River Glyme—Park, Outer and Inner—Mr. Wise—Sir W. Chambers—Gardens at Blenheim—Italian, Chinese, American Public Gardens—Père Benoist—Mr. Fortune—Washington Irving on Oxford Scenery.

EXETER DINING HALL.

THE trees at Blenheim are very grand, and however they may be arranged, succeeding summers will bring them out in their glory. But the view of the palace is really pleasing as we enter the park; and, at any rate, the freedom with which it is opened to the public tends to enlist any visitor's sympathies.

Those were fortunate who visited Blenheim before the year 1861, and saw the Titian Gallery, for in that year it was totally destroyed, with all its contents; but these related to a style and belonged to subjects with which our sympathy becomes less every day. There was a painting of Neptune and Amphitrite; Mars and Venus; Apollo and Daphne; Vulcan and Ceres; Bacchus and Ariadne; Pluto and Proserpine; Cupid and Psyche; Jupiter, Juno, and Io;

Hercules and Dejanira, &c.; and the worst of this class of subjects is that they possess no historical value, no costumes, or other matters of interest, but are only the fancies of a painter.

Far more interesting are his portraits, especially when they represent such worthy subjects as the Doge Antonio Grimani. Here we have human forms and feelings, and not only the likeness, but the spirit of the sitter is reproduced. The Doge is represented as seated against the background of a dark wall, partially relieved by hangings. This portrait is one of Titian's greatest works, and has been excellently described in a recent work on the great painter's life and genius. Speaking of this picture, the writer says, "his gaunt head and grand toothless jaw seem worn with every kind of care, yet still prepared to defy them all; while his eye seems as if it is scanning in the distance the fatal battle of Sapienza, which produced for him dishonour, fetters, and exile."

But the pictures at Blenheim hardly convey a pleasant impression of art, though there are, doubtless, many very fine ones. Such pictures, however, as "Seneca bleeding to Death," with the reddening tint of the water in the foot-bath finely rendered, are not such as we dwell over for long; or the picture which the little work on a tour in England, previously alluded to, speaks of as the "Earl of Strafford's Secretary reading his Death Warrant" is, from an artistic point of view, rather too painful. This title is not correct, for it really is Lord Strafford dictating to his secretary before his execution. The picture is a marvel of genius: the highly-wrought face of the victim—and that not a prepossessing one—and the more refined but blank look of the secretary, are wonderfully told. This picture was painted in duplicate by Vandyck, and the original, at Went-

worth House, in Yorkshire, is even finer. It has not been my
lot to see it, so I borrow Macaulay's description :—

"But Strafford : who ever names him without thinking of
those harsh, dark features, ennobled by their expression into
more than the majesty of an antique Jupiter; of that brow,
that eye, that cheek, that lip, wherein, as in a chronicle, are
written the events of many stormy and disastrous years, high
enterprise accomplished, frightful dangers braved, power un-
sparingly exercised, suffering unshrinkingly borne ; of that fixed
look, so full of severity, of mournful anxiety, of deep thought, of
dauntless resolution, which seems at once to forebode and defy
a terrible fate as it lowers on us from the living canvas of
Vandyck?" And in another place Macaulay writes: "Portraits
which condense into one point of time and exhibit at a single
glance the whole history of turbid and eventful lives—in which
the eye seems to scrutinise us and the mouth to command us
—in which the brow menaces, and the lip quivers with scorn—
in which every wrinkle is a comment upon some important
transaction. The account which Thucydides has given of the
retreat from Syracuse is, among narratives, what Vandyck's
'Lord Strafford' is among paintings." This description I only
read after seeing the picture at Blenheim; but though the other
one at Wentworth is, doubtless, a still greater picture, there
is much in this one to arrest attention; and probably it will
remain in the recollection as long as any at Blenheim, though,
perhaps, hardly pleasantly; nor can the distance of time since
the event, even aided by the circumstance that Strafford was
inimical to the liberties of the people, lend it much enchant-
ment. There are many portraits of the Marlborough family of
great interest in the house, by Kneller, and Reynolds, and
others. Some of Sir Joshua's finest works are here, especially

the well-known family group; and though there is a sameness in his faces, and he is so far below the grasp of Vandyck, it is not a just criticism which says he was greater with his pen than his pencil, excellent and all-instructive as his lectures are.

There is a general disappointment at the comparative smallness of the rooms in Blenheim. The state drawing-rooms are high and rather well-like; they have almost a prison effect from the interior, and the saloon, which communicates with the great hall, is perhaps hardly improved by the portraits of figures of different nationalities that are supposed to be looking down admiringly on the guests. One group, by way of outdoing the most zealous symbolical designers of the day, represents the first Duke of Marlborough in a Roman soldier's dress, arrested in the career of victory by Peace; and symbolism can hardly go further. However, we have now nearly passed through such conceits: a portrait painter is not required to read up his classics to supply him with costumes, and a man may, in all human probability, be able to point to his dining-room walls and say, "My father in his habit, as he lived!" An aldermanic chain, or a deputy-lieutenant's coat, or the full regalia of a mason, may be the glorious apparel in which it has pleased him to be taken; but if they are real, by all means let the fullest range be allowed to select any suit from a wardrobe—that is his own affair, and none of ours; besides which, a carefully-painted official dress may be of some historic value. But why a man like Reynolds should paint Lady Charlotte Spencer in the character of a gipsy, telling her brother—Lord Henry Spencer— his fortune, is not apparent; though this is more excusable than Kneller painting Sarah Jennings as Minerva. There might be some excuse, perhaps, for altering the costume of a sea-captain who paid a hurried visit to Bristol, or Liverpool, or Hull. Tailors might not be at hand to supply him with a proper suit; or his sea-legs might present obstacles. He might appear as Jason, or Triton, and the artist, perhaps, relieved from some difficulties, especially if we consider that the audience for whom the portrait was intended would not be hypercritical, and would allow him some latitude in the item of mythology. But Kneller and Reynolds have no such plea to urge in their defence; they both of them knew a great deal better than to represent their sitters in strange attire. But there is in Blenheim, some would think, rather an excess of the artificial surrounding; and as allusion was made to Eaton, it is almost impossible to refrain from making some comparison. Eaton Hall is on a much greater scale than Blenheim, and its apartments are finer. But with all that the feeling of comfort and homeliness has never been lost sight of; and it looks like a house to *live in*, though possibly the charges at which it stands would go very far indeed towards the building of two Blenheim Palaces; at least, that is the common belief. And I can hardly refrain from making one more allusion. The ceiling of Blenheim entrance-hall is nearly twenty-five yards high, and at this vast height Sir James Thornhill has represented Victory crowning Marlborough as she points out the field of Blenheim, and by way of being conspicuous, the duke is clothed in a blue Roman tunic. At Eaton, in the hall, however, a much more modest group prevails for the eye to rest on. It is an early king in the middle of a group of statuary settling some disputed limit of land, which he decided against the house of Grosvenor.

The lake at Blenheim is a very notable feature, and is formed by damming up the river Glyme, which thus floods some low lands, and forms in addition a cataract. This river rises in

Heythrop Park and Chipping Norton, and runs through Kiddington Park, Glympton, and Wootton, till it enters Blenheim. It turns a great number of mills on the way, and has many scenes of quiet rural beauty. It is rather unsuitable in many respects for supplying a large ornamental lake, owing to the great numbers of lilies and rushes its waters produce. Some compensation may be found for this in the abundance of wild fowl that are always floating on its surface. But the fish are of the coarser kind, and instead of trout and grayling we find huge pike, and chub, and bream. Still, there are many pleasant scenes on it, and the one here shown, with the two bridges, is an interesting, wild-looking spot, rarely disturbed, at most times of the year, except by an adventurous tourist or a solitary gamekeeper. This lake also receives a constant rill of clear water from Rosamond's Well, which rises at the foot of a rock, and is received into a clear basin, from whence it flows into the lake. Near the well was the palace of Rosamond, which was built for her by Henry II.

The park at Blenheim is on a very grand scale indeed. From Wootton Wood to Bladen, the distance, measured in a straight line, is three miles, and its breadth from Woodstock to the east end is nearly a mile and a half. In its form it is an oblong, and it contains about two thousand seven hundred acres. This would rank among the largest of the private parks in England. There are some few larger, but only a few.

In spite of all strictures, it is a very pleasant park, and many are the delightful walks in it through dense avenues, and past trees of gigantic and erratic growth. The river Glyme, which runs through it, divides the park into two. The outer portion is generally spoken of as the Great Park, and the inner

THE LAKE, BLENHEIM.

part is the lesser park, and in this the private gardens are situated.

It would seem that these were commenced during the building of the palace, and entrusted to Mr. Wise, who was very commonly employed by the royal family, and enjoyed the reputation of being a great man.

But these gardens occupy a very large space—some three hundred acres in all; and though his name does not appear in any chronicle at hand, it would seem probable that Sir William Chambers had something to do with them. This is more probable from the circumstance that Chambers built the Town-hall at Woodstock—at the cost, it is said, of the Duke of Marlborough—a structure on which his fame, happily, does not rest.

The gardens at Blenheim are divided into various parts. There is, for example, the Italian Garden, the Rustic Garden, the American Garden, the Rock Garden, and the Public Gardens, &c. &c.; and though this variety of design is not quite in accordance with modern ideas, there can be no doubt of the grandeur of the scale on which these various gardens are laid out. Some of the scenes in the Rustic Garden—where there is a view of the valley, and where large trees are placed in the most convenient and appropriate places for effect—are extremely beautiful.

The Italian Garden is simply an attempt to introduce the style we see in Italian palaces; and effective enough though these are, it is not a difficult matter to contrive them.

The Chinese Room also, with Cromwell's tea-pot, and the great collection of curious pottery—some of the specimens being the spoils of Marlborough's campaigns—is rather appropriate for the purpose for which it was erected.

The American Garden is planted chiefly with trees and flowers from the West. In that quarter of the world—in the northern parts, at least—it may be worth noticing that the flowers have hardly any scent, and the birds no song, excepting a few short, sharp, harsh notes.

The guide-books will tell, much better than I could pretend to do, of the great fountain designed by Bernini—the last work, as it is said, in which he was engaged, and that was a copy of one designed by him and erected at Rome ; and of the obelisk that stands on stones thrown together apparently at random, and occupying the centre of a large basin. Also of the wonderful Portugal laurel, which measures more than a hundred feet from branch to branch; the many plants of all nationalities that fill the crevices in the Rock Garden; the golden yews, yellow chestnuts, and scarlet oaks of the Rustic Garden ; the rosary and the pinery, and the grand cascade that bounds the lake, which was designed by Capability Brown. They will tell of the temples and aviary, and of all the delights which are to be found in the public and private gardens.

In some respects the Public Gardens would command most admiration : they have more connection with the outer world. We are enlivened with glimpses of Handborough Church and the great dense woods of Wytham, of Bladon Tower, and the White Horse Hill. How delightful all these old names are! Indeed, I have heard people who have passed some years abroad say that a Bradshaw's Guide, with the list of stations, reads to them almost like an epic poem. I have seen a colonist warm over a Warwick guide or time-bill, and say he felt like a countryman of Shakespeare again.

It may not be amiss, while on the subject of gardens, to allude to the general belief, long in existence, which credited

China with being the great centre of horticulture. Père Benoist, writing in 1745, says: "Je suis arrivé à Penkang, sous le tetre de mathématicien. . . . Les Chinois dans l'ornament de leurs jardins employent l'art a perfectionner la nature. Ces ne sont pas, comme en Europe, des allées à perte de vue—des terrasses, d'ou l'on découvre dans le lointain une infinité des magnifiques objets, dont la multitude ne permit pas à l'imagination de se fixer sur quelques-uns en particulier. Dans les Jardins de Chine la vue n'est point fatigueé parce qu'elle est presque toujours bornèe dans un espace proportionné à l'étendue des regards." And so the *père* proceeds to describe a real Imperial Chinese garden, which, seeing that he was a guest of the Emperor's, is probably correct enough, though it must be feared he thought that all Chinese gardens were on an equally splendid scale.

Mr. Robert Fortune was commissioned by the Horticultural Society to go to the Flowery Land and collect specimens so far back as the year 1843, and he somewhat dispels the idea which Sir William Chambers had held, and many others since him, that all good landscape gardening must come from the Celestial Empire. We are indebted to the Chinese for the peony and chrysanthemum, and the azalea and camellia, it is perfectly true, and when grown wild in vast tracts, as they are there, they are very imposing. He says that most people admire greatly the azaleas which appear annually at the Chiswick *fêtes,* and in single instances they quite equal the best specimens that grow in the land of their fathers ; but this gives only a faint idea of the gorgeous beauty of "azalea-clad mountains, where on every side, as far as our vision extends, the eye rests on masses of flowers of dazzling brightness and surpassing beauty." Nor is it the azalea alone which claims our admiration :

clematises, wild roses, and honeysuckles, and a hundred others, make us confess that China is indeed the central Flowery Land.

But in their cultivated state the Chinese flowers are not so attractive; nor could Mr. Fortune penetrate as far as Soo-chow-foo without difficulty and danger; this, however, he managed at last to do by assuming the Chinese costume; but the simple-minded Chinese were generally a match for him. He offered on one occasion to give ten dollars for a yellow camellia, and one soon came to hand, in bud. The florist had an old ticket on it, in Chinese characters, and Mr. Fortune took the precaution of getting this translated by a native merchant, who said it was a certificate that the plants produced yellow flowers—one deep yellow and the other pale. On another occasion he was closely beset by curious natives, who crowded round him to see his specimens and note-book; but he felt a hand in his pocket, and turning quickly round, saw a Chinaman making off, whom he pursued; but as the man threw away an envelope with a list of plants in it, he picked it up, wondering at the fellow's simplicity in taking what was useless to him. In the case of the flowers, however, when they bloomed they were common camellias; and the simple-minded Celestial who threw away the paper did not at the same time throw away a purse which left Mr. Fortune's pocket along with the piece of paper.

There is a description of the Emperor of China's autumnal garden at Yuen-min-yuen (or "eternal spring") by Mr. Barrow, who was attached to the Chinese Embassy, and who saw more of it than any other man; but he shall speak for himself. It must be recollected all the while that these gardens are about the size of Blenheim Park, or some ten or twelve miles in circumference. "He thought it a delightful place : the grand

and agreeable parts of nature were separated, connected, or arranged in so judicious a manner as to compose one whole, in which there was no inconsistency or unmeaning jumble of objects, but such an order and proportion as generally prevailed in scenes entirely natural. No round or oval, square or oblong lawns, with the grass shorn off close to the roots, were to be found anywhere in those grounds. The Chinese are particularly expert in magnifying the real dimensions of a piece of land by a proper disposition of the objects intended to embellish its surface. For this purpose, tall luxuriant trees of the deepest green were planted in the foreground, from where the view was to be taken, whilst those in the distance gradually diminished in size and depth of colouring ; and in general the ground was terminated by broken and irregular clumps of trees, whose foliage varied, as well by the different species of trees in the group as by the different times of the year in which they were in vigour ; and oftentimes the vegetation was apparently old and stunted, making with difficulty its way through the clefts of rocks either originally found or designedly collected upon the spot. The effect of intricacy and concealment seemed also to be well understood by the Chinese. At Yuen-min-yuen a slight wall was made to convey the idea of a magnificent building, when seen at a distance through the branches of a thicket. Sheets of water, instead of being surrounded by sloping banks like the glacis of a fortification, were occasionally hemmed in by artificial rocks seemingly indigenous to the soil."

Sir William Chambers was an architect of some ability, and a good traveller as well. He went to China as supercargo at an early age ; indeed, he returned when eighteen years old, but in that time he seems to have made some use of his opportunity to investigate Chinese gardening and architecture. He published a book, indeed, on the latter, which is occasionally seen in old book catalogues for sale. His best-known works in England were Somerset House and some buildings for Lord Bute, who had the highest opinion of his talents, and procured Government commissions for him. He also erected a house for Lord Clive at Claremont, and was extensively engaged for Lords Bessborough and Abercorn; and in the city he built houses for Lord Melbourne and Lord Gower, the one at Whitehall and the other in Piccadilly. He had several pupils who became notable: one of them, Gandon, built the Custom-house at Dublin, which is so conspicuous an object in entering the Liffey; and another was Thomas Hardwick, who had a considerable reputation at one time in England.

The Town-hall at Woodstock is, of course, a building that would be passed by, or perhaps the village builder of the period might be debited with it; but the Temple in Blenheim has more merit, and if style can indicate the designer, certainly he was the architect for the Temple of Diana in Blenheim Gardens. The following is the way in which he describes his own observations—or, if we were disposed to be very nice about a word—impressions of Chinese gardens. He did not publish his work until thirty years afterwards, and then it is shrewdly supposed that he had elaborated much of it during the interval, for his actual observations at seventeen can only have been small. Nevertheless, his work attracted great attention at the time of its appearance, and it was considered that Chinese gardening should be the model for English imitation. There can be little doubt that we see his hand at work at Blenheim. The first extract is from his dissertation on Oriental gardening; and the rest is from the pen of Sir George Staunton, who had an opportunity of seeing the Emperor's Summer Palace in Taiku :—

"The usual method of distributing gardens in China is to contrive a great variety of scenes to be seen from certain points of view, at which are placed seats or buildings adapted to the different purposes of mental or sensual enjoyments. The perfection of their gardens consists in the number and diversity of these scenes, and in the artful combination of their parts, which they endeavour to dispose in such a manner as not only separately to appear to the best advantage, but also to unite in forming an elegant and striking whole." Again, "Such is the judgment with which the Chinese artists situate their structures [in their gardens], that they enrich and beautify the particular prospects, without any detriment to the general aspect of the whole composition, in which Nature appears almost always predominant; for though their gardens are full of buildings and other works of art, yet there are many points from which none of them appear, and more than two or three at a time are seldom discovered, so artfully are they concealed in valleys, behind rocks and mountains, or amongst woods and thickets."

This Oriental picture is summarily dismissed by Sir John Davies :—

"Sir W. Chambers' description of Chinese gardening," he says, "is a mere prose work of imagination, without a shadow of foundation of reality. Their taste is, indeed, extremely defective and vicious on this particular point; and, as an improvement of nature, ranks much on a par with the cramping of their women's feet. The only exception exists in the gardens at Yuen-min-yuen, which Mr. Barrow describes as grand both in plan and extent; but for a subject to imitate these would be almost criminal, if it were possible."

The following extract is from Sir George Staunton's reliable account of Zhe-hol, the Emperor's summer residence in Tartary :—

"The party stopped at a number of small places near the water's edge, there being no considerable edifice. There were other buildings erected on the pinnacles of the highest hills, and some buried in the dark recesses of the deepest valleys. They differed in construction and ornament from each other, almost every one having something in the plan of it analogous to the situation and surrounding objects. . . . Figures in stone of a few animals stood in a flower-garden, besides monstrous and disgusting lions and tigers in porcelain, before several of the buildings. . . . In continuing their ride, the party found that the grounds included the utmost inequality of surface—some bearing the hardy oaks of northern hills, and others the tender plants of the southern valleys. Where a wide plain happened to occur, massy rocks were heaped together to diversify the scene; and the whole seemed calculated to exhibit the pleasing variety and striking contrast of the ruggedness of wild and the softness of cultivated nature. The gardens were enlivened by the movements, as well as the sounds, of different kinds of herbivorous animals, both quadrupeds and birds, but no menagerie of wild beasts was perceived. Some monstrous varieties of gold and silver fishes were seen playing in ponds of pellucid water, upon a bottom studded with pebbles of agate, jasper, and other precious stones. Throughout these grounds they met no gravel-walks, no trees planted in belts nor collected in clumps. Everything seemed to be avoided which betrayed a regularity of design. Nothing was observed to be directed, unless for very short distances, by straight lines, or to turn at right angles. Natural objects seemed scattered around by accident, in such a manner as to render their position pleasing; while many of the works of human labour, though answering every purpose of convenience, were made to appear the produce of rustic hands, without the assistance of a tool. Some of the elegancies and beauties which are described as taking place in Chinese gardens were not perceived by the present visitors; but the gardens of Yuen-min-yuen, near Pekin, from whence those descriptions are chiefly taken, are supposed to be more complete than those of Zhe-hol."

Now, this subject of Chinese gardening is very interest-ing, and I am tempted to dwell upon it, as it seems to give a key to many of the devices at Blenheim and some other spots round Oxford where Chambers was employed.

An ancient Chinese writer, Liew-tschew, asks what it is that we seek in the pleasures of a garden; for he says that some amends should always be made to men for living away from their more congenial dwelling-place free and

THE MARLBOROUGH COLUMN.

unconstrained. "The art of gardening," he says, "consists, therefore, in combining cheerfulness of prospect, luxuriance of growth, shade, retirement, and repose, so that the rural aspect may produce an illusion;" and it is said by Humboldt that similar ideas are propounded, so early as our own Norman Conquest, by an eminent Chinese statesman. But according to an "Essay on Chinese Gardens," written in 1782, the enthusiastic author says that the best European gardens, compared with the Chinese, only remind him of the Eclogues of Fontenelle as compared with those of Virgil.

The taste for such luxurious domains, he says, is of great antiquity, and from the reign of Tcheaw, or six hundred years before the founding of Rome, down to the seventh century of our era, the pleasure-grounds of Chinese Emperors were almost as great a feature as preserving game in vast forests was to the early Norman kings. One garden is said to have been 150 miles in circumference, and others were little inferior ; but these belonged to the Emperors only, and private gardens were forbidden. Thirty thousand slaves were employed in one imperial garden ; and as if to illustrate how far a vicious taste could go, there were artists engaged to weave flowers and leaves of silk, and to scent them with artificial perfumes, when the natural ones had paid the debt of nature.

Perhaps most persons will agree that the artificial decorations of Loudon and Wise, which were to a great extent copied from Le Nôtre at Versailles, left too little to nature; and the Dutch gardening of William that prevailed at the same time was no improvement. Yews and box-trees were cut into the shape of peacocks or quadrupeds, and walks

were trimmed into the straightest and most formal shapes.
There was a reaction against this, and Kent and Brown,
with many others, decided to crush out everything that
did not look like nature, and to twist even natural objects,
from anything like regularity; and to instance how the
maxim, " Ars est celare artem," could be caricatured, it is
said that Kent actually had dead trees put into Kensington
Gardens. Now with relief we turn to a description of English
park scenery from the pen of the accomplished American writer,
Washington Irving; and this description was written after a
tour in Oxford amongst the very scenes we are describing :—

" Nothing can be more imposing than the magnificence of English park
scenery. Vast lawns that extend like sheets of vivid green, with here and
there clumps of gigantic trees heaping up rich piles of foliage; the solemn
pomp of groves and woodland glades, with the deer trooping in silent
herds across them, the hare bounding away to the covert, or the
pheasant suddenly bursting upon the wing; the brook, taught to wind
in natural meanderings or expand into glassy lake; the sequestered
pool, reflecting the quivering trees, with the yellow leaf sleeping on its
bosom, and the trout roaming fearlessly about its limpid waters ; while
some rustic temple or sylvan statue, grown green and dark with age,
gives an air of classic sanctity to the seclusion.

" These are but a few of the features of park scenery ; but what
most delights me is the creative talent with which the English decorate
the unostentatious abodes of middle life. The rudest habitation, the
most unpromising and scanty portion of land, in the hands of an
Englishman of taste, becomes a little paradise.

" The sterile spot grows into loveliness under his hand ; and yet the
operations of art which produce the effect are simply owing to cautious
pruning and the nice distribution of flowers and plants of tender and
graceful foliage ; the introduction of a green slope of velvet turf; the
partial opening to a peep of blue distance or silver gleam of water :
all these are managed with a delicate tact, a pervading yet quiet
assiduity, like the magic touchings with which a painter finishes up a
favourite picture.

" The residence of people of fortune and refinement in the country has diffused a degree of taste and elegance in rural economy that descends to the lowest class. The very labourer, with his thatched cottage and narrow slip of ground, attends to their embellishment. The trim hedge, the grass-plot before the door, the little flower-bed bordered with snug box, the woodbine trained up against the wall and hanging its blossoms about the lattice, the pot of flowers in the window, the holly providentially planted about the house to cheat winter of its dreariness, and to throw in a semblance of green summer to cheer the fireside : all these bespeak the influence of taste, flowing down from the high sources and pervading the lowest levels of the public mind. . . The effect of this devotion of elegant minds to rural occupations has been wonderful on the face of the country. A great part of the country is rather level, and would be monotonous were it not for the charms of culture; but it is studded and gemmed, as it were, with castles and palaces, and embroidered with parks and gardens. It does not abound in grand and sublime prospects, but rather in little home-scenes of rural repose and sheltered quiet. Every antique farmhouse and moss-grown cottage is a picture ; and as the roads are continually winding, and the view is shut in by groves and hedges, the eye is delighted by a continual succession of small landscapes."

This has more of the right ring about it; we seem to breathe more freely here than among the stifling perfumes of the East. In all our descriptions of the Chinese gardens there is a heavy-loaded odour. We are expected to be astonished by some polite house-proud host, and to be perpetually on the stretch of admiration. But in such scenes as Washington Irving describes no apology is wanted, and without any effort we can enjoy every season of the year. A park or garden in winter has many charms, and the empty branches often open out new views that were hidden in summer-time.

At the beautiful park of Crichel, in Dorset, English gardening alone has been cultivated, and the old-fashioned flowers—Canterbury bells, geraniums, snapdragons, violets, roses, and suchlike—have been cultivated almost exclusively

in the gardens and greenhouses, each one being developed
to its highest degree.   Indeed, indigenous flowers and fruit
are more capable of being brought to a high standard in
their own soil than exotics.   Compare a first-class garden-
rose with a wild one, or a "Blenheim orange" with a crab-
apple; and there is no doubt that if blackberries had been
taken in hand in good time we should have had these
fruits as large as apricots a very long time since.

MERTON GATEWAY.

CHAPTER XI.

"And Cæsar's spirit, ranging for revenge,
　　Shall in these confines, with a monarch's voice,
　　Cry, 'Havoc!' and let slip the dogs of war."—*Julius Cæsar.*

Marlborough's Pedigree—Marlborough as a Leader—His Place in History—Addison's Poem
—Charlbury—The Roman Villa—Circumstances of its Discovery—Roman Occupation of
England—Roman Baths and Aqueducts—Sacking of Roman England—Mosaics—Baldon.

GABLE AT ST. ALDATE'S, OXFORD.

THE Duke of Marlborough's father, Sir Winston Churchill, was descended from an old family in Dorsetshire, and went at an early age to St. John's College, Oxford, but he left on account of civil commotions, and never obtained a degree, although his progress in literature was very conspicuous. He engaged in the civil wars, and took the side of the King, but suffered in his future for this very severely. In the year 1663 we find that he was knighted by Charles II., and that soon after he became a Fellow of the Royal Society.

The summit of his earthly prosperity, however, seems to have been a commissionership in the Court of Claims in Ireland, and he was also, whatever it may mean, a Clerk Comptroller of the Green Cloth—a hazy title that probably conferred some valuable revenues which, putting the case mildly, were on the liberal side for requiting any services done. When he was

thirty years old, his son John was born at Ashe, in Devonshire, and he was instructed in the rudiments of literature by a
country clergyman till he went to St. Paul's School. He was
considered rather fortunate in having a pair of colours given
to him in the Guards through certain backstairs influences on
which it would not be very pleasant to dwell. Even at the
early age of twenty-two he began to show great aptitude for
the military service, and the Duke of Monmouth, who said
he was much indebted to the prowess of Captain Churchill,
reported his success to his father.

He afterwards opposed the Duke of Monmouth on his
landing, defeated and captured him, and had him brought to
execution. Then he was entrusted with a command to defeat
the Prince of Orange, but he joined him instead. There are,
of course, many different accounts of his career as politician
and diplomatist, but some of his moving impulses will in all
probability never be known. He seems, however, from the
first to the last, to have made many enemies; and if the
singular history of the building of Blenheim, and the most
discreditable attempts of his enemies, were fairly to be taken
into account, as shown in their endeavours to thwart his
plans, not only in the field but also in private life, there is
every reason to hope that the great general might find a very
strong advocate.

I saw, some time since, in a review of some work, that
comparisons between men were fit to please schoolboys with—
that such things always seemed to arrest their attention, and
they were fond themseves of indulgling in such speculations.
The remark was perfectly just and true, only I must add that
such employment is both useful and instructive. Here we
bring men to their levels, as in a large public school every

one is sure to find his ; for, however much one may excel, he will be certain at one time or other to meet with those who excel him in many things of which he was proud before.

The exact place that Marlborough should occupy among great captains has often been a matter for speculation; and though it would be difficult to make sufficient allowances for circumstances to enable us to compare him with Cæsar or Hannibal, the materials of war were nearly the same in his time as they were in Napoleon's or Wellington's. Now, of course, they are in every respect entirely different—steam, rifled guns, and breech-loaders have altered the whole conditions of warfare, albeit the last-mentioned is, by the way, an older invention than it is sometimes supposed to be. It dates back, indeed, to the days of Agincourt, and would doubtless have been generally employed long since, but it was put aside as useless by Government.

There is much in the personal character of Marlborough which we as Englishmen shrink from ; and, happily, his vices —duplicity, to which he added, it is to be feared, even treachery also—were not those of his countrymen; always supposing that they could fairly have been laid to his charge. Again, he was so ungratefully received by his contemporaries after his battles were over, that it is quite possible some of his shortcomings may have been magnified by his political enemies; and on his return to England after such battles and victories as Malplaquet and Oudenarde, it is wonderful that he met with indignity and insult from his countrymen. " Six millions of supplies," St. John wrote, " and the country fifty millions in debt! The High Allies have been the ruin of us." Yet all this was written, not on any single ground on which, if six millions were proposed for war purposes in our day, such an application would probably be opposed, but simply in party spirit. The theory that there might be a distant war, with England merely a sad spectator, would in those days have been received with scorn and derision; and all parties agreed that if there should be any quarrel without England coming at once to the front, and taking one side or the other—it little mattered which—she would lose the respect of Europe.

This is mentioned to show how even his brilliant successes failed to secure for him the affections of the people; and the probability is that if we were better acquainted with all the matters of fact, we should smooth down some of the asperity of our judgment of the man; and this I am induced to believe from certain letters which I have read in the historical manuscripts published by the Government in blue-book form.

As far as his character as a captain or general—or by whatever other name it is called—is concerned, I have no hesitation in saying that many persons who consider all his circumstances would call him the very greatest the world ever saw, or, at least, greater than any one that we could possibly form a judgment of. He seems to have had an intuitive genius for war: not matured by experience like Wellington's or Napoleon's, or, indeed, any other great leader's; for he had held no important command till the eagle eye of William reluctantly pointed him out, while on his death-bed, as the only man who could guide the Grand Alliance. He had spoken of Marlborough—one fears, not without reason—in more bitter terms than he ever used towards Louis, the oppressor of his native country; and we sometimes feel a regret that the William to whom we all owe so much never lived to see the justness of his advice. Events of vast moment were gathering in clouds round Europe; and he plaintively told his favourite minister that he had seen the time when the change he felt coming over him would have been a welcome issue out of all his afflictions and sufferings, but now, he said, "I own I see another scene, and could have wished to live a little longer."

As for Marlborough himself, he seems, with such scanty training as we know he can only have had, to own no rival in military genius. He had to contend with Tallard and Villeroy, and many other great leaders, who had been men of war from their youth, and he suddenly appeared on the scene, and not only won battle after battle, but he did so with the most consummate ease. His enemies proper—that is to say, those against whom he fought on the field of battle —were in reality his least trouble. It was his allies—and, indeed, his own countrymen—he had to contend with. Yet Voltaire says of him that he never besieged a fortress he did not take, nor fought a battle he did not win. There seems to have been always such a reserve of strength about him that he inspired a sort of sympathetic activity in his men, who went over Europe with him, appearing in any unlikely place where he required them ; and he was so calm in the fiercest battles that one pardons Addison's poem written in his praise.

Poems to generals are always things we are apt to pass by. Some benevolent philanthropist, or perhaps some hard-working, self-denying man who gives up his leisure, without reward, for the benefit of others, may be quite a proper subject for a poem, and the verses might be read with pleasure ; but anything on a general is liable to appear bombastic.

Take, for example, the following poem of Addison's as an apt illustration :—

> "But, oh ! my muse, what numbers wilt thou find
> To sing the furious troops in battle joined ?
> Methinks I hear the drum's ambitious sound
> The victors' shouts and dying groans confound !
> The dreadful bursts of cannon rend the skies,
> And all the thunders of the battle rise.
> 'Twas then great Marlborough's mighty soul was proved,
> That, in the shock of changing hosts unmoved,
> Amid confusion, horror, and despair,
> Examined all the dreadful scenes of war
> In peaceful thought; the field of death surveyed,
> To fainting squadrons sent the timely aid,
> Inspired repulsed battalions to engage,
> And taught the doubtful battle where to rage.
> As when an angel, by divine command,
> With rising tempests shakes a guilty land,
> Such as of late o'er pale Britannia passed,
> Calm and serene he drives the furious blast ;
> And, pleased the Almighty's orders to perform,
> Rides in the whirlwind and directs the storm."

The only thing that saves this description from the charge of bombast and exaggeration is the simple fact that it is really not an exaggerated picture of Marlborough during a battle. Then all his calmness and coolness came to his aid, and though the one on whose word the issues depended, he was the least moved in his army. Men saw him in the midst of the battle giving his words of command with "indolent ease," and always ready to lead any charge in person, if he thought it was required. He was recognised at once as the head of the Grand Alliance by all parties, and met the phlegm of the Dutch and the pettiness of German princes alike, and the opposition of his officers and the libels and detractions of his countrymen, with the same calm indifference.

Yet he not only took his position as a commander suddenly, and without the progressive steps that are always regarded as necessary, but he did that, too, when many men think they may begin to look forward to retirement. When Marlborough first took a command he was older than Wellington was when he fought the battle of Waterloo.

Any one will be amused, if not gratified, at reading in old records and state papers relating to the Duke of Marlborough the history of the building of Blenheim. The Queen had already promised to build at her own expense a palace at Woodstock to be called Blenheim, and during the administration of Lord Godolphin the sum of £200,000 had been granted as royal warrants. This sum was quite inadequate, and the new ministers endeavoured to throw all the cost of finishing Blenheim Palace on the Duke himself, by endeavouring to obtain from him or the Duchess a promise to indemnify the contractors; but Sarah Jennings was quite the wrong person to be entrapped in such a manner, and stopped the works in the year 1710, and the Treasurer simply had them secured from damage during the ensuing winter. In the spring of the following year, however, a further sum of £7,000 was obtained in consequence of a warrant granted by the late Treasurer, Lord Godolphin, and Sir John Vanbrugh applied to Lord Oxford for a further advance towards completing the national monument. Very unwilling he was to comply, but he knew the Queen's word had been pledged, and he was constrained at last to require the architect to furnish him with an estimate of all that was required, and Sir John readily acceded to the most reasonable demand. From this it seemed

that £87,000 was all that was required, and the Treasurer was
quite delighted to think that this was all; but even then
estimates were sometimes exceeded.   However, on the 17th of
July, the Treasurer obtained the Queen's sign-manual for
£20,000, the original warrant for which sum, signed "Oxford,"
is preserved at Blenheim, and the architect was assured that
the further grants would follow as soon as possible.   On this
Vanbrugh wrote to the Duke of Marlborough :—"I acquainted
the chief undertaker with what had passed at the Treasury ;
upon which encouragement they went on with their work,
without insisting that all the money then issued should go
in discharge of the debt, which otherwise they would have
done."

But the building continued to occupy the attention of
Government; "for on the 25th of June, 1713, an estimate
was laid before the House of Commons of the debt on the
Civil List, due at Midsummer, 1710, amounting to £511,762.
One of the items was the sum of £60,000, by estimation for
the building of Woodstock."

Of course this latter sum should have properly been applied
to paying the debt on Woodstock, but only £10,000 was so applied; and that at the end of the session, when the Queen was
indisposed, and Oxford wished to conciliate Marlborough.   On
the accession of the new sovereign, Marlborough directed Sir
John Vanbrugh to form a complete estimate of what would
be required to finish Blenheim completely, and that architect,
after careful calculations, stated that £54,527 4s. 2d. was the
necessary sum; but this, he said, would include the bridge over
the Glyme, and laying out and planting the gardens, but it
does not seem to have included the park walling, and several
other necessary works.

This estimate, however, was laid before Parliament, and Marlborough's enemies succeeded in their unworthy attempts at delay till better counsels prevailed, and it was urged that as the Queen had undertaken the responsibility of paying for Blenheim, the nation could not refuse supplies; and accordingly an Act was passed " for enlarging the funds of the Bank of England, and for satisfying an arrear for work and materials at Blenheim, incurred while the building was carried on at the expense of her late Majesty."

It is perhaps not generally known that a considerable sum of money was owing on the house after the parliamentary grants had been exhausted, and the contractors sued the Duke himself for the amount. The case came before the House of Lords, and it was decided against the Duke on the singular grounds that Sir John Vanbrugh acted as his agent; and as he signed the plans, which of course is customary among all architects, he was bound by his agent's acts, and must pay. He appealed to Chancery, but with no better success; for after hearing the case, Lord Macclesfield confirmed the decision. During this protracted event, however, the Duke died.

If, when we leave Woodstock, we walk over to Handborough Station, near Blenheim, we are not very far from the celebrated Roman villa that was discovered some few years since; but this is, perhaps, hardly the best way of approaching it from Oxford: it serves for a very delightful day's excursion by itself. It is better to take the train to Charlbury, on the Oxford and Worcester line; then we shall be within about four miles of our destination.

The first object that will strike us on landing from the train is Charlbury Tower, which stands boldly out on the opposite side of a deep gully, through which the Evenlode

brawls on its way to the Thames. The church is principally Perpendicular in style, but there are some few older
parts, and in the yard is a magnificent yew-tree. Charlbury
is a large village, with broad, clean streets. The houses are

HANDBOROUGH.

very substantial in appearance, and it strikes a visitor as
curious to see so many of the entrances paved.

Few persons will know what you want if you ask for
the "Roman villa," but the road to it is very easily found.
Inquire for Fawler or Ashford Mill, and everybody will be
able to direct you. Still keeping along the broadest road,
you pass by a quarry, which is shown in the Ordnance
map correctly, but opposite to it is marked a road that

leads directly to the Roman villa. There is some error here; the villa is in the next gully, and the road is about three-quarters of a mile past the quarry. It must be remembered, however, that in this journey it is not safe to calculate upon finding any one of whom to make inquiries about the road.

The scenery is delightful. As soon as we have left Charlbury, we pass a fine old-fashioned country house, called Lee Place, with a roomy lawn and large elm-trees; and if we turn to the right we have a fine view of Wychwood Forest and Cornbury Park. Cornbury Park at one time formed part of one of the vast demesne forests of the king, which covered nearly eighty square miles, and was devoted entirely to the beasts of the forests, of which the greater number are extinct; and the estate passed through some of the principal houses of England. At one time it seems to have belonged to the house of Bedford, and at another to the Dukes of Northumberland; afterwards it was the seat of the Earl of Danby, which name Evelyn in his Diary has singularly transmuted to "Denbeigh;" and after the Restoration it became the property of the Earl of Clarendon, who took his title of Viscount from it; so that it may be said to have passed through an abundant variety of owners, till in 1751 the estate was purchased from Lord Clarendon by the trustees of John Duke of Marlborough, and it is now in the possession of Lord Churchill. Skelton says—"The mansion is of great beauty and interest. It contains, besides a handsome, spacious hall, many apartments of fine proportions. Contiguous to the hall is a chapel of pleasing proportions, and highly decorated with rich carving in wood. There is an excellent collection of pictures, judiciously disposed in the various chambers, amongst which are several fine portraits." There is an unfinished picture of Charles II., painted by Rubens, and several of the Marlborough family, by Sir Godfrey Kneller. There are also some extremely beautiful crayon drawings by Gainsborough, and a very extensive and valuable collection of the old masters.

A stream which rises in the forest of Wychwood is converted into a number of large fish-ponds, which extend for nearly a mile along the south-eastern part of the park. Much of the forest is under cultivation at this end, but the remoter parts are still a wilderness. The road undulates most beautifully, and many are the shapely trees and groves that skirt the path and dot the valley. For a country of such beauty and, apparently, productiveness, the inhabitants are very few indeed, and the desirability of remembering to have a proper understanding of the road before leaving Charlbury will soon be apparent; though it is true we pass the hamlet of Fawler, about two miles from Charlbury. The scenery here is perfectly delightful, and a vast green slope, bordered and studded with elms, and oaks, and beeches, is an ideal model of a site for a residence. The stillness of the valley is only broken by an occasional train that rushes below on its way to Worcester. After passing a lane end which leads to Stonesfield, the road dips into the valley and passes Ashford Mill, and then the quarry is reached, and the road which takes us to the villa; and it may be well to add here that if it is proposed to return to Oxford on foot the route may be changed by going through Bladen and Begbrook and Wolvercot. This leaves Eynsham on the south. But if the train is preferred, it is not at all necessary to return to Charlbury; we can take a pad road from the Roman villa, and a few steps will land us on the

Oxford and Worcester railway track. There is a pathway by this for foot-passengers, and Handborough station will be reached by a walk of two miles.

It was a little surprising to discover that so few visitors find their way to this villa. Just one or two strangers from London, or some other distant place, I was told by the woman on whose farm it was, or a very occasional resident of Oxford, and only three students, had paid her a visit in the course of a year. Yet the wonders of this villa are only half explored, and the ploughman exposes coins and relics as often as he turns over a field. There must be many floors yet also that are concealed by sods, for the villa covered between two and three acres, without making any allowance for such outbuildings as may have perished.

The discovery of this villa was very simple, and, according to Skelton, it was in this wise. The Roman road called Akeman Street runs along the northern boundary of North Leigh. From time to time bricks and tiles of a peculiar form had been discovered, and a suspicion gained ground that extensive remains were not far off. There was in the field that has been described a square enclosure, where the sods were higher than the natural level of the soil; and it seemed probable, at the first view, that these indicated some vast quadrangular building.

This building lay only a few feet from the surface, and little by little its grand proportions were laid bare to the inspection of the astonished spectators. Among the rooms that were discovered was a well-proportioned one, thirty-three feet long and twenty broad, the walls of which are more than three feet thick. This room was divided into two nearly equal parts by piers, which supported an arch;

and the fallen stones, cut to a *voussoir*, show that such was their original use. Many of these arch-stones had been cut out of the bases of columns, or other parts of older buildings; and from the *débris* found in clearing the floor it was evident that the chamber had been vaulted. " The ceiling had been finished with a coating of very fine thin plaster, formed into compartments by red, blue, and green fillets on a cream-coloured ground, and decorated with the foliage of the olive." The sides of the room seem to have been finished in a similar manner, and the colours were very rich indeed. In many parts of the room a skirting remains, formed of pounded brick, and extremely hard. It is two inches and a half in thickness, and is in the form of a quarter circle. Above the skirting the wall was coloured a dark Etruscan brown, to the height of six inches; then there was a narrow fillet of white, another of brown, and above them the plaster was of Etruscan yellow. The walls were lined with square brick funnels, which communicated with the hypocaust. Some flues were evidently for warm air, while others of larger calibre were disfigured by smoke.

Room after room is traceable in this wondrous structure, but not all are yet examined; and they would seem to correspond with the general plan of a great Roman villa. But there is sufficient evidence, from the hypocausts which have been uncovered, to show that the mansion was to be occupied in different parts during summer and winter.

Some dry stone walls of a rude construction, and differing in every particular from the splendid masonry of the palace, cut one of the rooms up in different parts; and there are the remains of fires on floors, which show with sufficient clearness that at one time it formed the dwelling of some rude class of inhabitants, who utilised its ancient walls.

In 1815 the north side of this interesting quadrangle was examined, and a suite of rooms was found connected by an interior gallery, which was about 170 feet long and ten feet wide. These rooms were one after the other laid open ; and from time to time the remains of a hypocaust, a very curious bath, and some rooms with coarse tesselated pavements, were found. In 1816 the western side was examined, and new rooms of great beauty were discovered.

The tesselated pavements are formed in simple, bold devices, not unlike some of the finest that are manufactured in Staffordshire or Shropshire ; but the method of laying them is many times more costly. Again, all the colours are all the natural tints of stones or marble. The *tesseræ*, or tiles, also are very small—two of them would scarcely cover a single square inch ; yet, for all this, the work has been executed with such incomparable care and skill that the floors are as true and even as if they had just been laid. What the cost of such a floor as this would be in the present day it would be impossible to say. Men would have to be drilled into the work and superintended by very careful foremen. But one thing is certain : if we consider that it is built over a hypocaust, and that there are beds of flags, and grouting, and filling, each of which has to be hardened and levelled before the tiling commences to be laid, the sum that would be required for one floor would build a large modern mansion.

I hope to see at some future time a popular account of the Roman occupation of great Britain. Remains enough are left to show how grand their empire was during their brief stay.

It is among the most astonishing chapters in history, and to us it should be the most interesting. Now we have Roman buildings, and Roman maxims in our laws, and many articles in daily use are designed from Roman models ; but these are not handed down from our Roman ancestry. All that was Roman completely disappeared from the island soon after the colonists so suddenly left, and for more than a thousand years a totally different kind of art and law and custom prevailed. The astonishing part of this Roman epoch is that it was so very Roman and yet so brief. Perhaps no colony was more completely Romanised than our own island, even among all those that the Empire subdued. Roman roads traversed the country in every direction, and we may still walk over hundreds of miles of Roman engineering. Legions were trained and drilled, walled cities of vast strength were built, and costly mansions rose in every county in England, yet the home of more than one Cæsar has left hardly any light upon its internal affairs or history, except what we can gather from colossal masonry, vast military earthworks, and costly pavements. We have some few inscriptions that speak of municipal or fiscal magistrates—triumviri or quatuorviri— but what they were we are left in provoking ignorance of—

> " They are ' vanished '
> Into the air, and what seemed corporal melted."

For all this, however, Roman remains show how thoroughly the invaders had subdued the island. Julius Cæsar's conquests, it must be remembered, dated some half a century B.C., and for nearly a century after that the Romans paid little attention to this country. They took home an evil report of the land, and the histories tell us that even the veteran soldiers were afraid of facing again the perils of the waters and the terrors of the unknown country. It was fully a century after this, when Ostorius Scapula defeated poor Caractacus, that they began to push their civilisation into our island; and it was in the latter half of the first century that the able general Suetonius pitched his camp on the site of Chester.

Now, if we remember that the Romans entirely left the island soon after the year 400, we may arrive at some slight idea of their energy as settlers. Take for example the front of a college—say University or All Souls; these do not carry one back into any considerable antiquity, yet they represent a period equal to the founding, flourishing, and decay of Roman rule. In that time they had carried Watling Street from Richborough to Anglesea, back again to Hull, and westerly once more to Carlisle. Ermine Street went from London to Lincoln, and it may be traced beyond that until the track is lost; the Fosse from Bath to Lincoln; and Icneld Street from Norwich to London. Now, these roads traversed more than 1,200 miles, and were formed in great part through trackless forests. They were not corduroys or plank roads, like our own colonists are so fond of constructing, but so excellent that we may say Telford himself could have taught the designers but little; and they are in use even to the present day. The mortar they employed in their buildings was so durable that it has been imitated by railway contractors for masonry where great strength is required, and is incomparably superior to that used by our own architects, even though made of almost the same materials. The system of warming the houses, though too costly for modern dwellings, had every known advantage to recommend it. There has been no villa discovered without a hypocaust, or floor supported on little slender shafts, through which heated air circulated, and the lasting heat this would give, even long after the fires had gone down, would fit the dwelling for the exotic strangers from the south. The floor was very substantial: a row of tiles was laid on the shafts, a bed of concrete on these, and tiles and concrete over that again.

The baths, both public and private, were constructed on the same plan as those of ancient Rome, or, in a word, more luxurious than those now to be met with in England; and some of their appliances in these have been copied, and even converted into lucrative patents, in modern days.

We may wonder, so far in vain, what relation our island bore to Rome. Did they look on British Romans as country cousins, who might once in a lifetime visit the great city? For the journey was of almost as great duration as in the present day would be a voyage to any of our colonies, and much more perilous. Or was it, as has been often said, the prize of the capitalist and the training-ground of the most reliable legions?

Certain it is that the occupation was not merely military. The remains point to a totally different conclusion; for it has been remarked that at Caerleon, York, and Chester, the headquarters of the second, sixth, and twentieth legions, there are not many costly pavements. These occur in profusion at Lincoln and London, which were not military centres; and sometimes the ploughshare lays bare some splendid floor away from any known Roman road or station. It is in the more remote places that marbles, both white and coloured, appear, and afford us a pretty sure proof of the tranquillity the island enjoyed. I have seen pavements that contained 2,000 *tessellæ* in every square yard. But all this wealth of design was left

suddenly as legion after legion was recalled to prop the
tottering Empire. Did the luxurious civilians make common
cause with the soldiery, and do their duty to the state? or
had they so far failed to conciliate the people in the country
parts that when the soldiers left they too vanished like
guilty things upon a fearful summons? Certain it is that
the Romans, both military and civil, left suddenly, and,
though surely there are remains enough to tell us much
more than we know, we are almost obliged to content ourselves with the words of Cassius—

"They are fled away and gone,
And in their steads the ravens, crows, and kites fly o'er our heads."

The sacking of Roman England, indeed, was complete, as
hordes from the north and pirates from the Elbe and Baltic
closed in upon the defenceless Britons, and compelled them
despairingly to send to Rome for the aid they had been so
long accustomed to. And one of the most pleasing circumstances we have to record is that they did not send in vain,
though this help could only be temporary; for Alaric, after
passing an inglorious Thermopylæ, had devastated the fertile
fields of Phocis and Bœotia, and was already quite on the
wrong side of the Alps. And now all is chaos; we are in pro-
found ignorance of the history of the island, though, indeed,
we know that the Roman remains met with no more mercy
than their prototypes in the great city. The invaders had
not one whit more reverence for them than a modern church
restorer has for an ancient abbey church. Gibbon, indeed,
gives a very unpromising account of the Attacotti, the
enemies, and afterwards the soldiers, of Valentinian. They
lived greatly by predatory incursions on the pastoral hordes

of the West of Scotland; but they preferred the shepherds and their families as articles of diet. "If," he adds, "in the neighbourhood of the commercial and literary town of Glasgow a race of cannibals has really existed, we may contemplate in the periods of Scottish history the opposite extremes of savage and civilised life." It was, perhaps, as early as A.D. 370 that Theodosius was sent from Rome to deliver Britain from these barbarians, and soon, as the historian tells us, he restored the splendour of the cities and the strength of the fortifications, and compelled, for a time at least, the northern hordes to retire to their old abodes. All this, however, was of short duration; the Britons were plainly told they must either look after their own affairs or succumb to their certain fate, which, indeed, was not far distant, and the time even had arrived when they could, during the brief lull, wander at will over the villas they had so often beheld with awe or worked at as slaves.

A vast number of Roman remains have been found in Oxford, and the three great roads pass through the county. It is often said that the Romans did not understand the simple fact that "water found its own level," and hence the great aqueducts that were scattered broadcast over Europe. Now, if the socket-pipes we use, and with which the Romans were perfectly familiar, were superior to aqueducts, there might be something to be said in favour of such a supposition, but the only advantage in conducting water across a valley by such means is its cheapness, and when that was weighed against stability, it is just the very advantage that the Romans would reject without one second thought.

Seneca remarks that "we are wont to make *dracones* and *miliaria* of many forms, within which we place pipes made of thin brass, coiled downward many times, surrounding the same

fire, in which the water flows through as much space as is
sufficient to make it hot. It therefore enters cold and flows
out hot;" and when we consider the number of patents this
has been the whole system of, it is rather arrogant to deny
the Romans the knowledge of water finding its own level.
Cardinal Wiseman, in an interesting lecture on the system of
Roman water supply, says (quoting from the *Building News*),
" As the Romans always brought their waters along a uniform
level, not only across the plain but through the city, where we
still trace them in the valleys between the hills, the aqueducts are beautiful objects while stalking across the country in
their naked simplicity; and so does the viaduct of a railway
become a graceful object in the landscape while connecting two
hills. But in passing or cutting through the midst of a city,
it is very different. Can any one imagine that the aqueducts
of Imperial Rome emerged into public sight or traversed the
Forum in grey peperino?" Most probably they did not, but
the floods of water entered the city through marble vestibules.
I only wish that the figures the Cardinal gives were sufficiently
accurate to justify their quotation here; but that in no way
must deduct from his interesting lecture, or the undoubted
fact, that the Roman sway, wherever it was, made an abundant
supply of water imperative. There can be no doubt that the
importance which the Romans attached to this subject, and the
regularity of their daily ablutions, was one principal cause of
their physical superiority over all nations with whom they
came in contact.

Dr. Lingard mentions a winding aqueduct five miles
long, which was connected with the great Roman wall, and
if we consider this wall for a moment, it will give us some
idea of the grandeur of the settlers.

Perhaps not many of us have adhered to the opinion which we gathered from early school histories that it was a long, strong wall, with sentinel-boxes at intervals, where hordes from the north could be seen, and a temporary check given to them.   Few, however, really appreciate its magnitude.   It was a vast chain of fortifications, with a wide, deep fosse before it, stretching across the island.   There were castles or forts every mile apart, and at every four or five miles there was a military depôt, a walled station covering some acres.   These were all bound together by a great wall, and behind it were roads connecting various parts, and enabling the garrisons to concentrate their cohorts at any point under the cover of the wall.   There are baths, and columns, and vaulted chambers of great size and strength, and the "wall," in fact, resembles any other of the more modern fortresses, except, perhaps, in its stupendous magnitude; for from Bowness to Wallsend it measures seventy-four miles.   Where there is any difficult height near its course, it seems, as if in enjoyment of its superfluous strength, to make a *détour* to go over its summit.

The mosaics are not so elaborate in England as in some other countries, though many have been discovered at London, Bignor, Bromdean, Bath, and other places, equal in beauty to those of Rome or Herculaneum in design, and show even more genius; for, instead of the architects having marbles ready to hand of different colours, they adapted whatever they could find in the neighbourhood—brick and stone, or clay, coloured more or less by burning, or admixture of mineral substances.   These mosaics represent chariot-races, sporting scenes, tanks of fish, gods and goddesses, and, in fact, all the scenes that are found on the Continent, with some few others besides.

However, the day arrived when the Romans must return to their own land, and suddenly leave their cities, their splendid roads and palaces, to the slender mercies of tribes from the north, the east—and Irish history claims, from the west— with what result we too well know.

" Hostis habet muros, ruit alto a culmine Troja."

Of the difficulty in procuring reliable information regarding the chieftains or peoples of the early part of this era, I found a notable instance in a " History of Ireland." Some latitude in the matter of dates, the most unbending, churlish Saxon would allow. Most of us would be indulgent to excess, probably; but when we have admitted, for example, that Ollamh Fodhla, as the historian whose work is before me declares, was " the most celebrated of the Irish kings," and " the reality of his existence is fully attested " (which no man of common prudence would dispute), we have fairly done as much as can be expected, especially as the author proceeds to say that while some authorities would bring his reign down to the present era others date it back to the founding of Rome, and others again estimate it to have been about six centuries before that time. " He was," he says " like the course of a brilliant and rapid meteor which, shooting across the face of the midnight sky, sheds around it a glorious light, but is instantly swallowed up by the surrounding darkness." Some plodding Lingard might stand aghast at this epitome ; but we must be content, even in our own Hengist and Horsa, with at least some parallel amount of metaphor.

A Roman road led from Oxford to Dorchester, and passed through Nuneham.) The lines of that road are not, I think, exactly identical with the present road, but the direction is the same, while the deviations are, perhaps, but slight; and from thence it travelled on towards London.

This road leaves Baldon on the right-hand side, and here a number of Roman coins have at times been found. The common is a favourite resort of Oxford pedestrians.

AT BALDON.

CHAPTER XII.

NEW COLLEGE, OXFORD.

OF course, the principal attractions
round Oxford are generally supposed
to lie to the north, and west, and south;
and there is a belt of rather uninviting-
looking land in the east, in the immediate vicinity of the city; but beyond,
the country is perfectly charming.
Thame is about twelve miles distant
from Magdalen Bridge, and can be
reached by rail easily. There are stations also at Littlemore, Wheatley, and
Tiddington. The former is near Sandford, the next is at a very long country
village near Holton Park, and the last is the station for Rycote
Park, where there is a long mere, fully three-quarters of a
mile in length, and at times a great resort for wild fowl. It
was this neighbourhood that suggested Washington Irving's
delightful description of English country scenery; but long
before we arrive at Thame there are many scenes of beauty
from Littlemore; Garsington may easily be reached, though
there is only a saving of two miles between going this way

and walking from Oxford. Garsington churchyard is one of the most beautiful in England. The landscape is of great extent, and the woodland scenery perfectly enchanting. Toot Baldon, and all the woods of Nuneham, lie mapped out, and

GARSINGTON CHURCH.

in the distance is the great range of the Berkshire Hills. The church itself is interesting, and the clerestory lights, which are at uneven lengths, are circular, a form which has been sometimes objected to as having the appearance of a hay-loft.

The tower of the church is early, and the tower lights belong to the first part of the thirteenth century; the corbels resemble such ordinary ones as we see in early work in any part of Oxford or the counties adjoining. The open porch on the south side is very pleasant, but I am not quite sure how much of it is original.

The harvest was just gathered in, the last time when I saw Garsington Church, and the day in the declining summer was peculiarly bright. The distant fields were literally like frosted gold, sometimes lost in the dense woodlands, and appearing faintly, like a gold thread in a velvet garment. I never remember to have seen such vast congregations of birds— starlings and fieldfares—which had come to fatten on the gleanings. They were not merely in thousands, but in hundreds of thousands. The rectory of Garsington is very valuable, and is in the gift of Trinity College, Oxford—the College of Pitt, Landor, and Bampton. Grinling Gibbons, who carved the beautiful wood-work in Trinity College Chapel, often used to repair to Garsington churchyard to enjoy the contemplation of its grand scenery.

The cross at Garsington has been destroyed, but the base is left, and is situated near some trees of great beauty.

Perhaps, however, there is nothing in quiet lane scenery in England to exceed in pleasantness the road up to Garsington, after the Great Western railway-bridge is passed, when the lane becomes very steep. The occasional cottages are primitive to a degree, and few are the wild flowers in England that do not flourish on either side of the road.

If, in place of taking the middle road from Oxford, we turn to the left after passing St. Clement's, we shall soon arrive at Headington. This is by the great Roman road that goes to Alchester and Bicester. The cross is the great attraction here, and is of considerable beauty ; the shaft is standing and in a state of good preservation. The church is an interesting old building, and the few external repairs do not seem to have spoiled its antique appearance. The actual cross that surmounted the shaft has been demolished for generations. Headington is, of course, only a short journey from the city, and easily reached in an afternoon, without effort.

But there is one of the many charming unchronicled places that I feel with dismay has been left out, and which must be brought into the *iter*. These places are, as I once heard an Oxford lecturer happily describe irregular Greek verbs, " like an unconquered country that rises on your march when you think you have subdued it." Instead of returning to Oxford by rail from Handborough, it is quite easy to extend the trip, either through South Leigh or Eynsham, to Stanton Harcourt, a residence of the Harcourt family : though here again, as in the case of the Roman villa, a special day is better ; and if we approach it from the city the best way is to go through Cumnor and over Bablock-hythe Ferry. The country in this way is very pretty, and contrasts strongly with the shorter way home through South Leigh, which is exceedingly dreary. Stanton Harcourt seems as we approach it to nestle in great shapely elms, through which moss-covered roofs are here and there visible, and among which the massive square tower of the church is seen and lost at intervals as we approach it. In the village the old stocks are standing, apparently in perfect working order ; and about a mile from it, on the ferry road, we shall notice the remains of a road-side cross, much grown up with grass, which relic dates back apparently to the fourteenth century. Nothing but the base is left. There is in the village a large cottage-like

A LANE AT GARSINGTON.

residence, which is used as a shooting-box by members of the Harcourt family, and some of the walls formed part of the ancient mansion; but some parts of the old residence are much more complete—notably Pope's Tower, or the tower which contains the room where he wrote the translation of Homer. This is very small—probably thirteen feet square—but with the exception of the height and the weary winding stone staircase, it is a pleasant room to study in, and its inaccessibility was an advantage to the great poet, for nobody excepting Gay ever intruded on his solitude. In the lower part of the tower is the chapel, and an opening is pointed out where one of the Harcourts used to listen to the services from his sick-chamber, which he occupied many years; the aperture was opened at service-time.

The view of the church is from the fish-ponds of Stanton Harcourt, and they still contain many heavy stone-fish.

A description of the kitchen is given from the Oxford Hand-book, and it may be well to remark, in addition, that the roof is carved. There are three ovens for bread and pastry, and the chief fire-place is sufficiently large to roast an ox whole. Though I transcribe the account of this kitchen, and though this is the generally received one, I must admit to feeling some little difficulty in supposing that the fires were originally in quite as rude a state as is said, and I cannot but think that at least there was some nearer approach to a chimney, especially as, within a few miles, there may be seen at Abingdon Abbey a very grand one, which collects the smoke, and is regarded as a perfect model.

" The walls are three feet thick; the room is square

below and octangular above, ascending like a tower. The fires were made against the walls, and the smoke climbing up the walls, without any tunnels or disturbance to the cooks, was stopped by a huge conical roof at the top, and escaped at loopholes on every side, which were opened and shut according to the direction of the wind. The height of the walls to the spring of the roof is thirty-nine feet. The roof rises twenty-nine feet in the centre. The outer walls are surmounted by a battlement." The kitchen is at some distance from the chapel, and the family residence occupied a space between them. Some of the outbuildings have been converted into a picturesque farmhouse. This was the principal seat of the Harcourt family until the early part of the seventeenth century.

In a pane of Pope's study at Stanton Harcourt, was an inscription to the effect that in the year 1718 he finished his fifth volume of the "Iliad;" but this has been removed to Nuneham, the present seat of the Harcourt family. Such a study, with its quiet, and in the middle of a lovely county, was Pope's delight. It is said that none, except his friend Gay, ever ventured to break in upon his solitude here; but his charm of manner, and his wit, and guileless nature, won the esteem of all that knew him. A remarkable memorandum is found on the back of a letter to Pope, which announced the death of his friend; Swift discovered it among his papers. "On my dear friend, Mr. Gay's death. Received December 15; but not read till the 20th, by an impulse foreboding some misfortune."

And Pope wrote the beautiful epitaph on his friend—

> "Of manners gentle, of affection mild,
> In wit a man, simplicity a child;

HEADINGTON CHURCH AND CROSS.

With native humour temp'ring virtuous rage,
Form'd to delight at once and lash the age ;
Above temptation in a low estate,
And uncorrupted e'en among the great ;
A safe companion, and an easy friend,
Unblam'd through life, lamented in thy end :
These are thy honours ! not that here thy bust
Is mixt with heroes, or with kings thy dust ;
But that the worthy and the good shall say,
Striking their pensive bosoms—HERE lies GAY."

Every one is acquainted with Pope's villa at Twickenham, and when we read a description of the garden there we have no difficulty in recognising the inspiration he derived from the Chinese taste of some parts of Blenheim. The distance would not be very great from Stanton Harcourt. Pope, of course, would ride, and his way would lie through Eynsham, Cassington, and Yarnton, to the Woodstock Road, which is entered between the fifty-eighth and fifty-ninth mile-stones from London ; Woodstock being distant four miles. A pedestrian, however, would find a much shorter, and a more interesting road over the hills, past Church Hanboro' and Burleigh Wood and water-mill. The following is the description of his garden spoken of above, and is from a letter addressed to Edward Blunt, Esq., of Maple-Durham :—

" I have put the last hand to my works of this kind, in happily finishing the subterraneous way and grotto ; I there found a spring of the clearest water, which falls in a perpetual rill, that echoes through the cavern day and night. From the River Thames, you see through my arch up a walk of the wilderness, to a kind of open temple, wholly composed of shells in the rustic manner ; and from that distance under the temple you look down through a sloping arcade of trees, and see the sails on the river passing suddenly and vanishing as through a perspective glass. When you shut the doors of this grotto, it becomes on the instant, from a luminous room, a camera obscura, on the walls of which all the objects of the river, hills, woods, and boats, are forming a moving picture in their visible radiations. And when you have a mind to light it up, it affords you a very different scene; it is furnished with shells, interspersed with pieces of looking-glass in angular forms; and in the ceiling is a star of the same material, at which, when a lamp (of an orbicular figure of thin alabaster) is hung in the middle, a thousand pointed rays glitter and are reflected over the place. There are, connected to this grotto by a narrow passage, two porches, one, towards the river, of smooth stones full of light, and open; the other, towards the garden, shadowed with trees, rough with shells, flints, and iron-ore. The bottom is paved with simple pebble, as is also the adjoining walk up the wilderness to the temple, in the natural taste, agreeing not ill with the little dripping murmur, and the aquatic idea of the whole place. It wants nothing to complete it but a good statue, with an inscription like that beautiful antique one of which you know I am so fond."

Some of Pope's correspondence with Lady Mary Wortley Montague, is from Stanton Harcourt. One in particular relates to the often-repeated tale of John Hewett and Sarah Drew being struck dead by lightning on the last day of July, as they sheltered under a beech-tree. They had been engaged for some time, and seem to have been greatly respected by their neighbours; and what made the circumstance more dramatic was, that it occurred only on the morning when John had obtained the consent of the girl's parents. Pope, in his letter, says that there was "heard so loud a crack, as if the heavens had burst asunder." And when the labourers, "all solicitous for each other's safety, called to one another, those who were nearest our lovers, hearing no answer, stepped to the place where they lay. They saw a little smoke, and after, this faithful pair—John with one arm about his Sarah's neck, and the other held over her face, as if to screen her from the lightning. They were dead!" He concludes by saying, "They were buried the next day, in one grave, in the parish of Stanton Harcourt, in Oxfordshire, where my Lord Harcourt, at my request, has erected a monument over them."

Pope wrote an epitaph, which stands yet at the head of the grave, and which is not worthy of him. It would seem that the "consent" of the parents was not considered indispensable by the ardent lover, for Pope says in his letter, "It was but till the next week they were to wait for the day to make them happy." And as the rubric says the "banns must be published in the church three several Sundays," they must have been twice read at the time.

There is another epitaph here, to the only son of Lord Councillor Harcourt, who was a friend of Pope's and a great patron of literature. It contains these lines—

> " How vain is reason—eloquence how weak !
> That Pope must tell what Harcourt cannot speak."

But while Pope was in his study at Stanton Harcourt, he had good friends working for him in London.

Kennet says that Dr. Johnson " happened to be in the ' coffee-house ' when Dr. Swift came in, and he had a bow for everybody but me, who, I confess, could not but despise him. When I came to the ante-chamber to wait before prayers, Dr. Swift was the principal man of talk and business, and acted as master of requests. Then he instructed a young nobleman that the best poet in England was Mr. Pope (a Papist), who had begun a translation of Homer into English verse, for which he must have them all subscribe. ' For,' says he, ' the author shall not begin to print till I have a thousand guineas for him.' "

It would be impossible to plot out our walks round the
grand old city more happily, than by taking an Ordnance
map to the promenade round the Camera Bodleiana, formerly the Radcliffe Library; or what is, perhaps, more convenient, a smaller district map, and reserving the particular
Ordnance map for the excursion. The walk is 100 feet
above the level of the street, and is 170 yards in circuit.
Not only does the city lie at our feet, but all the grand
woodland scenery in the surrounding neighbourhood is spread
out like a panorama. It is well to get hold of some old
Oxford inhabitant, and he will readily point out the various
localities. The view is, of course, very much the same as
that from Stanton Harcourt Tower. Just about the time
the camera was built, the landscape must have been enriched
by the noble front of Eynsham Abbey Church, which, to
judge from a drawing by Anthony Wood, seems to have
been of cathedral dimensions. It consisted of two great
towers, a west window with a door under, and two doors
under the towers—an arrangement we see in our largest
cathedrals, and one that was never employed on a small
scale. This drawing has been copied in the Lives of
Leland, Hearne, and Wood (Oxford, 1772), in the second
edition; and many copies can be consulted in the city.
It would doubtless be easy for any architect, by the
assistance of this, after making due allowance for the in-
accuracies and rudeness of the plate—and with the aid of
Dugdale, who gives it prominent place in his first volume—
to reproduce a sketch of the façade as it probably appeared. The records are kept in fairly good Latin, and I
think that with a little research, the dates of the buildings could be discovered as each abbot added to them.

So important a part does the Camera Bodleiana play, and so thoroughly is it identified with Oxford and its surroundings, that a slight sketch of the history of its founder might be in place here. The building was designed by Gibbs, who built Ditchley, and many other places round Oxford. He was greatly in demand for gentlemen's houses; and this is a good example of his style; and the play he had gave him every opportunity of showing his best points, for he was, perhaps, as little fettered here as anywhere.

John Radcliffe was born at Wakefield, in Yorkshire, in 1650, and educated at University College, Oxford, but elected to a fellowship of Lincoln. Dr. Marshall, Rector of Lincoln College, opposed his application for a faculty place in the college, which was to serve as a dispensation from taking holy orders, which he was required to do if he kept his fellowship. It is commonly said that Dr. Radcliffe acquired wealth and fame more by wit than by learning; and, indeed, it is quite possible, from all that is left of his memory, that he was not unacquainted with the way in which more modern practitioners have often made themselves sought after, and their utterances received as Delphic. "Where are your books?" once asked Dr. Bathurst, the President of Trinity College. "There," said the doctor—"that is Radcliffe's library," pointing at the same time to a herbal, and a few phials, and a skeleton. But he found that his genius did not lie in academic life, and resigned his fellowship in 1677, and in four years after became an M.D. and a "Grand Compounder," whatever such a formidable title may have meant. He resided at Bow Street, Covent Garden, and had for a neighbour Sir Godfrey Kneller. They were far too caustic in their own lines not to come into contact before long, and a doorway was the bone of contention. It seems to have led into a garden, and there was a difference as to its ownership. Radcliffe, however, suddenly gave up all claims to Kneller, if the other would promise not to paint it; and Kneller replied that, short of taking his physic, he would do anything to oblige him. He soon became "Grand Compounder" to Princess Anne of Denmark; but he lost his favour through his rough deportment, and it is said, also, by not always having his intellect perfectly clear and unclouded when he was sent for.

In 1699, William of Orange sent for him, to consult him about his swelled ankles, and his thin legs and body; and Radcliffe said, "I would not have your Majesty's two legs for your three kingdoms;" and though William was not the man to court flattery, this was rather more than he cared to put up with, and Radcliffe was paid off.

Godolphin, who spent much time at Blenheim, and was a favourite at Court, endeavoured to have Radcliffe reinstated at Court; but Queen Anne said, that if she sent for him, he would very likely send for reply, that "her ailments were nothing but vapours." On one occasion, when she sent for him to see her at Carshalton, he returned answer that he had taken physic himself, and could not come. He had a great regard and respect for the clergy, and he gave the living of Headbourne-worthy, in Hampshire, to the excellent and worthy Dr. Bingham. The advowson of this living is now in the possession of University College. The mastership, also, of St. Mary's Hall, was conferred, through his influence, on Dr. Hudson, and he it was who persuaded the doctor to bestow such magnificent gifts on the university.

Dr. Mead speaks in enthusiastic terms of Radcliffe, and says that on one occasion the doctor suddenly exclaimed, " Mead, I love you well, and I will tell you of a secret how to prosper in the world : use all mankind ill!" There was one trait about him that we should hardly have expected to find, and that was, his exceeding closeness in money matters. He could not be prevailed on to pay an account, even after it was due, without great difficulty, and frequently legal processes had to be served on him before the money could be got from him. At tavern reckonings also, he generally contrived to let his neighbour discharge the score, until his unwillingness to " change a guinea," as he used to express it, became proverbial. However, he has left his large fortune in a manner that has proved a boon to succeeding generations.

The difference between the Oxford of the present day, which this Library overlooks, and the Oxford of the period when it was built, is comparatively small; but, if we could, in imagination, transport ourselves to the Middle Ages, and see Oxford as it then was, what a contrast should we see! and how different from our elevation would the city appear. Now it is filled by "grave and reverend seniors," second to none, in scholarship and self-respect, in the world ; and the very fact of having even been a student there, is a passport over all British dominions ; but the scene it once presented was a very different one, and here we may be pardoned for quoting an extract from the "History of the English People," as showing the contrast between Oxford of to-day, and Oxford of two hundred years ago :—

"But to realise this Oxford of the past, we must dismiss from our minds all recollections of the Oxford of the present. In the outer aspect of the new university, there was nothing of the pomp that overawes the freshman as he first paces the 'High,' or looks down from the gallery of St. Mary's. In the stead of long fronts of venerable colleges, of stately walks beneath immemorial elms, history plunges us into the mean and filthy lanes of a mediæval town. Thousands of boys, huddled in bare lodging-houses, clustering round teachers as poor as themselves in church-porch and house-porch, drinking, quarrelling, dicing, begging at the corners of the streets, take the place of the brightly-coloured train of doctors and Heads. Mayor and Chancellor struggle in vain to enforce order or peace in this seething mass of turbulent life. The retainers who follow their young lords to the university, fight out the feuds of their houses in the streets. Scholars from Kent, and scholars from Scotland, wage the bitter struggle of North and South. At nightfall, roysterer and reveller roam with torches through the narrow lanes, defying bailiffs, and cutting down burghers at their doors. Now a mob of clerks plunges into the Jewry, and wipes off the memory of bills and bonds by sacking a Hebrew house or two. Now a tavern row, between scholar and townsman, widens into a general broil, and the academical bell of St. Mary's vies with the town bell of St. Martin's in the clanging to arms. Every phase of ecclesiastical controversy or political strife is preluded by some fierce outbreak at the Papacy. The students besiege a legate in the abbot's house at Osney. A murderous town and gown row precedes the opening of the Barons' War. 'When Oxford draws knife,' runs the old rhyme, 'England's soon at strife.' "

From the promenade we get glimpses, not only of the Thames, and Cherwell and Thames, but of the canals that run through Oxford and Berkshire.

The wharf-scene here shown is the termination of the Wilts and Berks Canal, and its principal, or perhaps its only, freight is English timber. The wharf is constantly full of it, and one would greatly regret the waste of sylvan beauty were it not for the fact that it is only by thinning the woods which abound in this part of England that shapely trees are grown. The stems would force themselves up in tall, lath-like forms, as we see them in the uncleared forests in America. The growth of English timber is slow; it is consoling to think that its place for economic purposes can be supplied in most cases from the enormous

BERKS AND WILTS CANAL.

forests of Canada and the shores of the Baltic. Some few articles which turners make for farm use, "elm knees" for ship-building, a little oak for furniture, and walnut for gun-stocks, are the only things now for which we are not dependent on foreign supplies of wood.

Canal scenes have a peculiar charm of their own, even

when they pass through a flat country.   Of course, the
Chester and Ellesmere Canal flows through some of the finest
scenery in the kingdom, especially when it runs on a bench
in the upper part of the Llangollen Hills, with the vale
far below, and stretching for miles through farms and
woods and parks.

But, far short of such advantages as these, canals have
many features that an artist loves.   The roads generally
cross them in steep bridges, quite unlike those over railways;
for when a road intersecting a railway is not of great
importance, a crossing and a pair of gates are sufficient—
sometimes, indeed, a crossing without the gates, if a gate-
keeper cannot be utilised for signals or shunts; and if the
road is of sufficient consequence it has had to be raised in
a gentle level before it reaches the rails.   The swing bridges
on a canal are not very numerous, and rather cumbersome
for general use, so that the bridges almost resembling those
on a willow-pattern plate have taken the rule, at least, in
the country parts.   In the lever bridge here shown there
is more than enough room for all the trees and their
branches.   The bridge is only moved to allow of the masts
which the barges carry when they navigate the Thames.
The total length of this canal is fifty-two miles, and it
joins the Kennet and Avon Canal near Shrivenham, in
Wiltshire, running in a north-easterly direction through the
vale of White Horse.

The Oxford Canal traverses that part of the county that
lies between Claydon, in the northern extremity of the
county, and Oxford.   It runs through the vale of the Cherwell, and in one part enters the river and utilises its
channel for about a mile.

Now, all these canals have plenty of objects of interest, if only we care to spend a summer's day in strolling along their banks, and the few notes I made in walking along them are almost as suitable for one part as another—as, for example, there is a memorandum of a sloping meadow that entered the canal with a steep bank grassed down to the water's edge, well filled with clean cattle, which took no more interest in a railway train that passed a few hundred yards off, with a horrible shriek, than of a canal boat that slowly laboured along by the towing-path. The latter seemed almost to excite more of their sleepy interest. Here and there, on the meadow side of the canal, a gnarled oak would stretch its branches over the water, and just clear the tarred funnel that reached down to the cooking-stove in the cabin, and did duty as a chimney.

Sometimes the meadow would dip into a tiny hollow, and the canal would fill it, and its margin would be belted with several yards of sedges, marsh foxtail, and rushes, but its surface scarcely aspired to entertain a water-lily— a very paradise for ducks, which, too generally, the farmer has neglected as not worth their keep, though in such a spot they would trouble him very little till, perhaps, the bells of St. Andrew's or St. Thomas's Day knelled out their approaching doom. Sometimes the canal would skirt a lawn, and mirror the forms of beeches and willows; while here and there a faint blue spire would appear in the horizon. The locks, again, are nearly always interesting and pic- turesque. In busy times two or three barges will be waiting their turns, and the horses either refreshing themselves from their tin cans or biting the grass on the side of the path; and a hundred picturesque groups can be made of them among the heavy white wooden levers and the exposed green gates.   The copings are worn into such deep ruts by the soft hemp ropes that one ceases to wonder at the geological changes a slight force can effect in the rocks, if only it is continuous and long enough.

But nowhere do canals show to greater advantage than in the basins in the towns they pass through.   There are Dutch-looking barges of many builds: some only intended for the still waters, and not rigged, while others are fitted out with heavy booms and cumbrous, old-fashioned wooden blocks for running tackle, which point them out at once as bound for ports at the mouth of the river.   The sailors— if they can aspire to the title—the crates of crockery or other manufactures, the undressed logs, and the tall, antique crane, rising up, form ever-varying pictures, quite equal to the scenes that Prout or any of his school have made themselves famous for.

Perhaps the picturesqueness and beauty are too often outside the barges; though, with their fresh-painted cabins and the thin blue smoke that curls out of the funnel, one would think that the life of a canal boatman was one of careless ease.   They go on the "ride and tie," principle—the one that walks by the horse begins to get a little tired of his work, and changes with the steerer, and when the locks are reached they can all be ashore together.   He is free from house-duty or rates of any kind, for his barge is his home, and no Chancellor has been so hardly pushed as to propose to extend the taxes to barge-cabins.   But it is to be feared, for all these advantages, that the actual life of a canal boatman might be much altered for the better. We read continually in papers of some police-case in which

OXFORD CANAL.

they figure not to advantage; and it often creeps out that they were born on a barge, and have slept on one for twenty or thirty years.

There is also a lingering interest about these canals, in their social and historic aspects, that often makes one pause and wonder what is to happen next. Only so far back as the middle of the last century goods were conveyed into Scotland on pack-horses, and the difficulties of the road may be understood, in that country, when Sir Henry Parnell relates that it took the ordinary carrier between Edinburgh and Selkirk a fortnight to complete his journey, though the distance each way was only thirty-eight miles; and in 1763 there was only one coach between Edinburgh and London, which started once a month from each place, and took a fortnight to complete the trip. And some time after this Arthur Young declared that the road between Liverpool and Manchester was so bad that he could find "nothing in the whole range of language to describe it;" and he "seriously cautions all travellers who may accidentally propose to travel it to avoid it." Some of the ruts after a wet summer were, he says, four feet deep, and filled with water; so what, he asks, would it be after a wet winter? In those days wagon-carriage from London to Leeds was £13 a ton, and from Liverpool to Manchester £2 a ton. Coals, of course, could only be transported where there was a sea-board; and many of the richest districts in England, both for coals and minerals, waited the advent of canals.

The energetic Duke of Bridgewater commenced his canal in 1765, and chose Brindley, a man of consummate ability, but all untrained, for his engineer. He it was who invented locks on canals, and fought down every possible obstacle that

could come in his way.   Wholly self-relying, he went to bed
in day-time to "think it over," when any great difficulty
presented itself.   But it was "like master like man."   The
wealthy Duke raised every shilling he could—and even
borrowed from every farmer who would venture his money.
On one occasion, when a cutting through very hard rock was
required, he is said to have taken out a snuff-box, and asked the
scared engineer if he could take that much rock a day, and
having of course an affirmative reply, told him to go on.   One
of his principles was never, if possible, to receive strangers on
business matters, however urgently they might desire to see
him.   "I will go," he said, "willingly to see them, for then I
can leave when I like; but if they come to see me, they leave
when they like."

The amazing success of this undertaking induced many
other lines, and England was soon covered with a system of
inland navigation, as we see it now.   Railways, of course, have
done much to reduce the value of canals; but for heavy goods
they must still be an important mode of communication.   But
what subjects for reflection canals are as we walk along them,
and how they show the sudden destruction that men may
bring upon themselves unawares!   The profits of canals grew
to enormous rates, and when rival lines were started they soon
amalgamated in common interest, and to extravagant charges
bad service was soon added.   It was proved in evidence that
cotton which had crossed three thousand miles of ocean in
twenty days often was six weeks on the road from Liverpool to
Manchester, and a tram-road was projected by merchants and
spinners to run in opposition; this was to be drawn by horses.
Yet even this excited great antagonism.   Gradually it was
proposed to employ stationary engines at different lengths of

the line to wind up the trucks; and after consulting the principal engineers, George Stephenson was answered with derision and ridicule by saying that he thought an engine could take a load at twelve miles an hour.

But canals might easily be made more useful than they are in reducing the floods that from time to time will blight the prospects of the farmer. This subject has been alluded to before, but in connection with canals it is hardly possible to avoid quoting one of the ablest authorities who have written upon this district :—

"The conditions which have to be taken into account, if thoroughly examined, might render a knowledge of the approach of floods a matter almost of certainty. It is, however, still a source of reproach that the possibility of their occurrence should be admitted above Oxford, as these inundations are directly the result of mechanical obstructions capable of removal. Indeed, certain alterations, and doubtless improvements, of late years have caused a few of our sanitary reformers to indulge in the hope that a flood in Oxfordshire had become merely a matter of history. Later experience must, however, have dispelled such a delusion ; and those who are not satisfied with evidences from *terra firma*, have but to look around from the leads of the Radcliffe Library to witness the great extent to which the inundations reach, affecting, as they do, not only the counties of Oxfordshire, Berkshire, and Buckinghamshire, but those of Northamptonshire, Gloucestershire, and Warwickshire, which supply the respective rivers of the Cherwell, Wenlock, Isis, Ray, Thame, Windrush, and other important watercourses of the Upper Thames valleys. Dr. Acland, about the year 1850, pointed out the serious natures of these floods in an able work, taking for his text, 'How much our climate affects the heads and hearts, especially of the finest tempers."

Where the Berks and Wilts Canal enters the Thames there are great beds of the beautiful flowering rush (*Butomus umbellatus*). It is a beautiful plant, with its graceful stem rising out of the shallow beds in the stream or growing along the edges. It is between three and four feet in

height, and is crowned with large clusters of flowers, purple
and white.   This plant is by no means, however, common
along the whole course of the Thames.   It is found in
abundance near Abingdon, and is also met with in large
patches near Dorchester, in the Tame.

There is another beautiful plant that is found on the
lock gates and old walls and woodwork near Abingdon in
great abundance : the ivy-leaved snapdragon (*Linaria cym-
balaria*).   It is a pendent flower, with deep-coloured leaves
resembling ivy, and curious flowers of a violet colour, not
unlike the common snapdragon, but very much smaller.   It
was originally introduced from Italy, and planted, it is said,
at Woodstock, whence it spread down the Glyme and Evenlode into the Thames.   It has, however, found its way
into many parts of England ; and though it prefers the
proximity of water, any old damp wall will suffice to find
it a home.   It is found in quantities on the city walls of
Chester, especially near the castle.

In conclusion, it may be remarked, on leaving these
pleasant scenes, that many places have not been noticed ;
and a heavy indictment seems to lie against me when I
refer to the map.   Some reflections have been indulged in
on many subjects, but these were for the most part such as
suggested themselves to our party in returning to Oxford after
visiting some point of attraction.

CASSELL PETTER & GALPIN, BELLE SAUVAGE WORKS, LONDON, E.C.